The

FIVE

Principles

Of

Powerful

Prayer

Margaret R. Banks

The Five Principles of Powerful Prayer
Copyright © 2009 by Margaret Banks

Cover design: Dean Harvey/De'Jean Thomas

ISBN (978-0-692-00793-8)

Printed in USA by 48HrBooks (www.48HrBooks.com)

In honor of my Lord and Savior Jesus Christ, I ask that you prayerfully meditate on His Words before you read mine. As you move through these pages, you will find a psalm opening each chapter of my book. I sincerely appreciate your interest in strengthening your prayer structure, and my prayer for you is that the Lord Jesus Christ would add to your life all his blessings that emanate from His Words into your heart and life.

Dedication

This book is dedicated firstly to my father - Kenneth George Banks – who went to his eternal reward when I was only nine years old. Dad I can still hear you say, "Margaret, have manners, it will take you through the world." Dad, if you can hear me, out of the many things that there are to do, I teach for the National Retail Federation as a Sales and Service Certified Trainer, neat don't you think?

Then to all my young people between the ages of 16-35, I have a great love for your souls, because you are the crown jewel for the Master, which makes you prime target of the enemy. Jesus said I call upon you young (wo)man because you are strong. You are strong to do what? I dare say to pray. Prayer should be viewed more as a verb as opposed to a noun. Your act of prayer will infuse worship that will take you far beyond your expectations. I submit to you that this is one of the reasons why the spirit of this world would like to have you, abuse you, and then discard you. I gave my heart to the Lord at the tender age of 14, and I fought every demon imaginable to get to where I am today. I can hear a young person say, *really*? Yes, *really!* I want to assure you that if I can make it thus far with the help of the Lord, you can too.

My prayer for you is that you give Jesus Christ a chance in your life, and "you", yes "you" will be surprised as to what He will make out of, and through your life. I implore you; take on the challenge to pray. I guarantee you, if you do, you will never go back to your old way of living again. Do you really want to be powerfully used by God? *PRAY*! God bless you. (*aight!*)

Table of Contents

Foreword

Dr. Stephen Sweeney, President of the College of New Rochelle, recently gave a reflective insight into the legacy of one of the College's finest- Sr. Dorothy Ann Kelly. In describing her contribution to the college he remarked- ***Divine Providence raises up champions; Providence provides the convergence, the congruence of gifts and talents to a particular historical moment.*** The success of this fine institution owes its existence to a faithful, gifted and legendary heroine who emerged at the perfect moment in the history and as such has impacted lives forever.

I feel compelled to draw a similar kind of parallel with the production of such masterpiece found in the production of this book. It comes to us at the perfect time in the history of the church and can best be described as the convergence of a Holy Ghost filled heart that has been unequivocally blended with the talents and skills of the author. We are truly blessed to be able to share such profound experience as well as to gain such powerful insight into the Power of Prayer. Those who have the opportunity to read the contents will never be the same again. Lives will be impacted, hearts will be blessed and our prayer lives will most definitely be enhanced.

In a society that has become so utterly self reliant, it is with a sense of joy that we proudly receive a relevant message, clearly equipping us with the worth and value of the greatest tool that a successful Christian will ever possess. The contents of this book will transport you to another realm where you will be enthralled by its message. May we welcome the new day that has dawned and embrace the message it brings to us. My sincere congratulations on a job well done!

Bishop Arthur Thomas
Oneness Rehoboth Apostolic Church

Acknowledgements

First, I must give all honor and glory to the head of my life, Jesus Christ the Righteous. I do publicly declare to my readers that Jesus Christ is my Center, my Circumference and everything in between. Life is over for me if Jesus is absent from my life. In addition, let it be known that I will not apologize or retract not one drop of my personal declaration, because I really love the Lord Jesus Christ!

To my mother, Vera Barrett-Haugabrook, I love you. In my estimation, you are one of the greatest women who ever graced this planet. You are a matriarch indeed. Mom I know you love the Lord, and as I grow older I see a great deal of your tenacity and strength seeping through my pores. Thank you *Mom* for being such a blessing!

To my five sisters: (Annicia, Cynthia, Silena, Karen, Denith,) and Tony, my only brother, thank you for believing in me. Special recognition to Karen for being my personal nurse in the hospital ordeal, heaven has your reward; and to Denith, even though you are deaf, you have such a heart of gold, I love you dearly!

To my pastor, Bishop Arthur Thomas, I owe my spiritual upbringing to you. You have taught me the true virtues of spiritual and moral values. Your leadership abilities are exceptional. Your positive and progressive approach toward academia has given me the courage to become a visionary and trendsetter. Your lifestyle mirrors Christ, and I am glad God allowed me the honor to serve at your table. May the Lord continue to prosper you and your family. This is my prayer. I love you sir!

Elesia Lawrence –Thank you so much for being there for me during and after my hospital ordeal. May the Lord's richest blessing rest upon you. Mouya Belford, my advocate, your reward shall be great! Andrea Williams, I believe you are one of the smartest women alive. Thank you for your encouragement and prodding. Your editorial and analytical skills were timely. Only heaven could do justice with any award I would try to give. Love you! Paulette Carty, I am indebted. Dean Harvey thanks for your encouragement. Your creativity and humility are coveted. De'Jean Thomas, your design of the five ball ornamented vine has given my book a touch of class; and let it be known that I would not have printed my book cover without your artistry. Success is definitely in your future. I decree it so and it shall be established, in Jesus' name. Amen!

Dr. Nyarko you are such an inspiration. The Lord sent you in my life just in time to aide me through the publishing maze. Could not have done it without your help. Thank you so very much!

Dr. Kesha-Gaye Anderson and Dianne Pusey, thank you for your time, effort, editorial skills and prayers. May the Lord continue to bless you with all spiritual and physical blessings that can only be found in Him!

Lastly, to all my prayer partners and friends, together we will destroy the works of the devil. Love you and a big Thank You for your enduring love, support and prayers.

Psalms 1

1. Blessed is the man that walketh not in the counsel of the ungodly, nor standeth in the way of sinners, nor sitteth in the seat of the scornful.

2. But his delight is in the law of the Lord; and in his law doth he meditate day and night.

3. And he shall be like a tree planted by the rivers of water, that bringeth forth his fruit in his season; his leaf also shall not wither; and whatsoever he doeth shall prosper.

4. The ungodly are not so: but are like the chaff which the wind driveth away.

5. Therefore the ungodly shall not stand in the judgment, nor sinners in the congregation of the righteous.

6. For the Lord knoweth the way of the righteous: but the way of the ungodly shall perish.

Introduction

The Power of Prayer

Never let God alone in prayer!
Vesta Mangun

Before we even attempt to talk on the subject of prayer, one must understand that you will not receive anything from the Lord without faith. The writer of Hebrews said, *"But without faith it is impossible to please him: for he that cometh to God must believe that he is, and that he is a rewarder of them that diligently seek him.*(Heb 11:6). And the Apostle James added: *If any of you lack wisdom, let him ask of God, that giveth to all men liberally, and upbraideth not; and it shall be given him. But let him ask in faith, nothing wavering. For he that wavereth is like a wave of the sea driven with the wind and tossed. For let not that man think that he shall receive any thing of the Lord.* (Jam. 1:5-7) EM Bounds admonishes: *In the ultimate issue, prayer is simply claiming its natural yet marvelous prerogatives, faith taking possession of its illimitable inheritance... Moreover, when faith ceases to pray, it ceases to live.*

The author and finisher of prayer is God! It is said that prayer, once set in motion never ceases to exist. In my humble opinion this is one of the truest statements ever uttered. With that understanding, one should never feel intimidated to make his or her request known before the God of heaven. Prayer is synonymous with supplication and worship, and is the channel that man uses to speak with his God. Prayer is the quickest route to getting God's attention. Prayer is a kingdom principle -- God's kingdom, that is.

Power on the other hand, is the force or authority that ignites and drives the pistons in the engine of availing and prevailing prayer. Jesus assured the disciples that they will receive *power* after that the Holy Ghost is come upon them, Acts 1:8. Power to do *what? Power* to step out of the natural and plunge into the supernatural! It is in this supernatural realm where the Christian wants to operate when he or she decides to follow and see the Lord Jesus Christ in His true glory. *For we wrestle not against flesh and blood, but against principalities, against powers, against the rulers of the darkness of this world, against spiritual wickedness in high places. (Eph.6:12)* May I declare that the real world *is* the *spirit* world!

So then, how can a mere human get the attention of this all powerful and sovereign God? The God directed answer is through Holy Ghost praying and fasting. Jude 20 mentioned, *Building up yourselves on your most holy faith, praying in the Holy Ghost.* The Holy Ghost is the guiding force that searches out and annihilates the forces of evil. The Holy Ghost infilling therefore is essential, especially to those who profess to be men and women of prayer, to empower them to continue Jesus' purpose and vision, which is to save souls and to destroy the works of the devil, as recorded in John 3:16 and 1John 3:8.

From the beginning of time, man had the inherent urge to talk with his God. We see in Genesis 2 and 3 that Adam and Eve though they faltered, held a premium on talking with God, which was evidenced in their son's lives. A similar desire was also reflected in the lives of their sons Cain and Abel, who in Genesis 4, came and presented their offerings or prayers to the

13

One whom they were taught would answer their prayers. Likewise, we see how much God yearned to talk with man that he developed such a friendship and fellowship with Enoch to the extent that one day while they spoke, the Lord took him home to heaven with him. (Gen 5:24)

Prayer like anything else is a learned behavior. Some people say prayers while others pray. A.W. Tozer alluded to that when he said, *"When we become too glib (smooth) in prayer we are most surely talking to ourselves."* Prayers that are rehearsed and recited are quite ok, since one must start somewhere. Then, there are prayers that are scripted, extemporaneous, and eloquently prayed with all piety. The attitude behind these kinds of praying is due diligence. Basically they are saying, I acknowledged the Heavenly Father today. But people who truly "pray," their prayers would be described as purpose driven, laced with a burden to effect change. They are heartfelt, framed and delivered with such passion and fervent intensity, that they move both God and man into action. These kinds of prayers will break the toughest of hearts and lead men and women into full submission to God. These prayers can only be prayed after one is endued with *power* from on high. This is what the Apostle Jude alluded to when he said *praying in the Holy Ghost*. The qualification, therefore, for praying like this is found in Acts 2:38. One should seek to be filled with the baptism of the Holy Ghost before you even attempt to get into authentic apostolic praying. Paul attested to that through visions and revelations, which he saw during intense prayer. He wrote of seeing things in the third heavens, which was not lawful for man to utter, as recorded in 2 Corinthians 12:1-4.

A story was told of a poor woman whose husband was near death and was no longer able to work to support himself or his family. So his wife had to fend for the family. One day, she

14

went to her local grocer and asked him if he could credit her some food until she was able to pay. Of course, the grocer was unaccommodating to her request, and ordered her out of his store. But the little lady had already prayed before leaving home and *"NO"* was not an option for her. She persisted with her request but the grocer only grew more angry and unrelenting.

In the store was a gentleman who overheard the conversation and told the grocer that he would be willing to foot the bill. He told the grocer to have the lady place her grocery list on the scale and whatever grocery the grocer believed he could give the lady, he should place it on the other side of the scale. To the grocers chagrin, the more groceries he placed on the scale it still did not outweigh the content on the other side. The list was much heavier. So he took up the grocery list, opened it and read it. With great big drops of tears, he read the list aloud. It read: *Dear Lord, please grant the grocer the heart to answer my request for the food needed to feed my family, in Jesus' name. Amen.* The grocer was so moved that he allowed the lady to take all of the grocery she needed without charging her a dime. I am not sure of the validity of the story but it is worth rehearsing. Never underestimate the power or weight of your prayer when prayed from a heart of sincerity and truth.

There are other categories of prayers that are chanted, read, and memorized by many religious groups; but, for the Holy Ghost filled believer, prayer is a divine call to ministry, the ministry of reconciliation. Prayer is the passport that grants believers full access to the throne of grace where they can find help in time of need. I would like to even take prayer a bit further than even finding help in the time of need, to make it the place where the believers dwell. The scriptures said in Psalm 91:1, *He that dwelleth in the secret place of the most High shall abide under the shadow of the Almighty.* Prayer then is one of the most, if not the most, fundamental privilege of the spirit-filled individual. The bible mentions in Rom 8:26...*Likewise the Spirit also helpeth our infirmities:* ***for we know not what we should pray for as we ought:*** but ***the Spirit*** itself maketh intercession for us with groanings which cannot be uttered.

Jesus commanded with such authority that men ought always to pray and not to faint in Luke 18:1. Jesus led by example. Let us review several incidents where the scriptures captured Jesus in the act of prayer:

> *Matthew 14:23 And when he had sent the multitudes away, he went up into a mountain apart to pray: and when the evening was come, he was there alone.*
>
> *Matthew 26:36 Then cometh Jesus with them unto a place called Gethsemane, and saith unto the disciples, Sit ye here, while I go and pray yonder.*
>
> *Mark 6:46 And when he had sent them away, he departed into a mountain to pray.*
>
> *Luke 6:12 And it came to pass in those days, that he went out into a mountain to pray, and continued all night in prayer to God.*
>
> *Luke 9:28 And it came to pass about an eight days after these sayings, he took Peter and John and James, and went up into a mountain to pray.*

It is incumbent, then, on all who would like to gain God's favor or friendship to adopt such passion for prayer. Prayer, I discover, is the best indicator of one's act of submission to the will and purpose of God. The Lord does speak to His own people in a manner that encourages surrender without a proverbial gun being placed to their heads. It is so reassuring to know that the God of the Universe takes time out to listen to a mere human pray...this is so heart stopping and exhilarating at the same time!

16

The purpose for this book is to create an avenue where the common reader will gain some perspectives on how to pray simple yet powerful prayers that will usher one into the presence of the Lord. Praying powerful prayers are not reserved for a certain segment of people, or to the lineage of a religious few, but are opened to all. Jabez, for instance, came out of obscurity, prayed a simple 33 word prayer that moved God to action. Today, unbeknownst to him, his prayer is still being prayed, books written without him getting any royalty, and has caused revolutionary changes in the lives of countless millions, simply because he prayed from a heart of sincerity and truth. So, you, dear reader, regardless of your level of spirituality, or church affiliation, will be able to apply at least one of these principles outlined in this book and begin a quest for a deeper relationship with the Lord through sincere prayer.

Along with insights for praying powerful prayers, I have included several testimonies and experiences gained through a life of prayer and dedication to my Lord and Savior Jesus Christ. The idea behind the title, the five principles of powerful prayer came to me during a prayer session, when I was asked to share a word of exhortation in our month of consecration in January 2009. In a simple frame, I will use POWER as an acronym to develop the five principles as shown below:

- *P*ray with Passion
- *O*penly Confess your Convictions
- *W*ork the WORD
- *E*xpect the Unexpected, and
- *R*emember, God Gets the Glory!

Let me take a few more minutes of your time to share a bit of what the process looked like to get this book to you. As indicated, there was a pressing need to write. The core contents took roughly 2 weeks to complete. During the process of writing and editing, a heavy burden of intercessory and apostolic praying would rest on me, coupled with a strong presence from the Lord. There were days when I wept and interceded as I tried to capture on paper what I believe the Lord had placed in my thoughts. So if you feel at times, while you read, that I am trying to engage you, it's because as I wrote I felt I was in conversation with you. Sometimes it might seem as though I am preaching, it is because I felt I was ministering to a body of people. Know assuredly though, that you were prayed for as I labored in prayer for those who would read these pages. I believe strongly that someone will gain insight, clarity and direction for ministry as s/he peruses through these pages. If this person is you, I pray that the Lord God Almighty and His holy angels will give you the grace to walk into your destiny; and as Mordecai said to Esther, *"And who knoweth whether thou art come to the kingdom for such a time as this?"(Esther 4:14)*

Thank you for indulging me as you read what I feel the Lord placed on my heart to help me first in my walk with Him, and to somehow aide you in your quest for Him. May our Lord and Savior Jesus Christ usher you into a closer walk with Him as you journey with me through these five principles of powerful prayer.

Psalms 141

1. *Lord, I cry unto thee: make haste unto me; give ear unto my voice, when I cry unto thee.*

2. *Let my prayer be set forth before thee as incense; and the lifting up of my hands as the evening sacrifice.*

3. *Set a watch, O Lord, before my mouth; keep the door of my lips.*

4. *Incline not my heart to any evil thing, to practise wicked works with men that work iniquity: and let me not eat of their dainties.*

5. *Let the righteous smite me; it shall be a kindness: and let him reprove me; it shall be an excellent oil, which shall not break my head: for yet my prayer also shall be in their calamities.*

6. *When their judges are overthrown in stony places, they shall hear my words; for they are sweet.*

7. *Our bones are scattered at the grave's mouth, as when one cutteth and cleaveth wood upon the earth.*

8. *But mine eyes are unto thee, O God the Lord: in thee is my trust; leave not my soul destitute.*

9. *Keep me from the snares which they have laid for me, and the gins of the workers of iniquity.*

10. *Let the wicked fall into their own nets, whilst that I withal escape.*

Chapter One

First Principle

Pray with Passion

"When you set yourself on fire, people love to come and see you burn."— John Wesley, **Evangelist (eighteenth century)**

Prayer is a *"passion"* that must be felt and not so much telt. The greatest people of our time who have impacted our lives in most cases are not aware of their effect on the lives of others. This statement stands true of the living legend that epitomizes the essence of what prayer looks like, feels like, and is. This is none other than the incomparable Lady Vesta Mangun, of the Pentecostals of Alexandria, from the great state of Louisiana. For over twenty-years I have read her work and listened to her preaching, and have adopted her style of fearless worship to the one whom she loves so dearly, our Lord and Savior Jesus Christ. Sister Mangun, you are my "Unsung Hero" and I do strive to emulate you as you so aptly stated, "Never Let God Alone in Prayer," at the Simply Jesus Conference, in Gaithersburg, Maryland.

Passion is a burst of energy that propels ordinary men and women to do the unthinkable and to reach extraordinary heights that were once known, only to a fortunate or I dare say the zealous few. Webster's New World Dictionary looks at passion from a different angle which I never even imagined or even conceived. He defines passion as *the suffering of Jesus during the Crucifixion or after the Last Supper.* He went on to say that passion is *any emotion such as hate or love; extreme emotion as rage, enthusiasm, lust, etc.; the object of strong desire or fondness.* The root word for passion in Latin derivative (*pati*) means – *to suffer.* Strong's Concordance defines the word to suffer in Greek as – (*pas'-kho, path'-o, pen'-tho*) - to *experience a sensation or impression (usually painful): - feel,* **passion**, *suffer, vex.* Time would fail to try and dissect this term in its entirety, (which could be a great subject for another book), but to think that Mr. Webster equated passion with suffering, pushes the pendulum to the next level of thinking.

In my quest to write this book I came across a book I purchased approximately ten years ago and felt a pull to read it. One section of the book based on prayer stood out to me and I would like to share it as an illustration of the power of a simple yet impacting prayer, which is prayed from the heart. After I read what the author went through, I wondered whether or not I was even worthy to write on the subject of prayer.

Richard Wurmbrand a Rumanian atheistic Jew, in his book "***Tortured For Christ***,[1]" published in 1965, tells of his conversion to Christianity. He spoke of how he was brainwashed as a youngster, and how the teachings and reading of Marx, Stalin, Voltaire, Darwin and others placed in his heart a hatred for Christ. He said, "*...not that I did not believe in God or Christ...I hated these notions, considering them harmful for the human mind.*" He confessed that he could not pass a church without feeling a pull to enter, but he never understood what was preached even after listening to the messages. Then one day he prayed a prayer that went something like this, "*God, I know*

---

[1] Tortured For Christ, 1965, 1967 by Richard Wurmbrand. Published by Diane Books, USA

surely that you do not exist. But if perchance You exist, which I contest, it is not my duty to believe in you; it is Your duty to reveal Yourself to me." At the same time, he later discovered on a mountain in Rumania, an old carpenter, who loved God wholeheartedly and had a passionate prayer life. He was impressed by the Holy Spirit to pray this prayer: *My God, I have served you on earth and I wish to have my reward on earth as well as in Heaven. And my reward should be that I should not die before I bring a Jew to Christ, because Jesus was from the Jewish people. But I am poor, old and sick. I cannot go around and seek a Jew. In my village there are none. Bring Thou a Jew into my village and I will do my best to bring him to Christ.*

Mr. Wurmbrand felt this irresistible urge to go that particular village out of the twelve thousand other villages in Rumania, and the catch was, he went there for no apparent reason, or so he thought. The old carpenter saw this as an answer to his prayer and ministered Christ to him. Mr. Wurmbrand went on to say that, the old carpenter gave him a Bible. He said he had read bibles before out of cultural interest but there was something special about this Bible. He remarked:

As he told me afterwards, he prayed for ***hours*** together with his wife for my conversion and that of my wife. The Bible he gave me was written not so much in words, ***but in the flames of love fired by his prayers.*** I could scarcely read it. I could only weep over it, comparing my bad life with the life of Christ; my impurity; my hatred with His love; and He accepting me to be one of His own…Soon after me, my wife was converted…

Richard Wurmbrand, whose body bears the scars of fourteen years of torture and suffering in a Communist prison, witnessed the indomitable courage and continuing faith of hundreds of Christian believers. Torn from his loved ones,

22

battered and beaten in body but not in spirit, they continue undaunted in their Christian faith even as they are TORTURED FOR CHRIST.

Are we ready then to suffer and to exude passion in prayer? Knowing the purpose for which He came, Jesus at the Last Supper, told Judas, whatever you do, do it quickly. Jesus was impassioned to complete his purpose. In the garden of Gethsemane, the scriptures said in Luke 22:44 *And being in an agony (pain, passion, suffering) he prayed more earnestly: and his sweat was as it were great drops of blood falling down to the ground.*

Only Jesus could have paid the ultimate price for the sins of man. There are many controversies around whether Jesus' sweat was actual blood, or if it was figurative, this writer will defer to the experts on the subject matter; however, there is one thing for sure, Jesus' prayer was intense enough to change the course of nature and to start a spiritual revolution that has stretched over two thousand years. What should be noted here is that for one to get to the next level of prayer, where the carnal man is completely mortified, one must be willing to pray until one presses through to a point of total submission even to requiring the release in your spirit that whatever you prayed for is done. It is all about pressing through the crud and darkness of this sin sick world, into a heavenly dimension to touch the face of the Lord Jesus Christ as it were.

Jesus agonized when he saw the travail of his soul, and what was in the cup of sacrifice. He asked the Father if He could take it away, but I am so glad that Jesus was able to press beyond the flesh, which was so weak, to fulfill the call of the spirit for which he came. Jesus' soul ultimately gained satisfaction as recorded in Isa. 53:11.

I think personality plays an important role in the manner by which an individual prays: Whether with a great show of emotion, loud and expressive, or controlled, subdued and calm, the most important thing to consider is not the "who" of prayer but the "how" of prayer. Kellogg's mascot, Tony the Tiger, would trigger questions if he ever said "GREAT" without the exclamation sign"!". Undoubtedly, passionate prayer will produce sweat, not focusing on perspiration per se, but the sweat that produces change to the inner man. When a man wears a t-shirt with the fitness guru's motto "No pain, No gain" across his chest, the observer's eyes immediately scans his physique to see if he is worthy of the saying. I dare say that we will be judged with similar criteria when we profess to be people of prayer, and there is little or no obvious sign that we have been with the Master. Case in point, the children of Israel were afraid to look at Moses when he came from meeting with God. "And it came to pass, when Moses came down from Mount Sinai with the two tablets of testimony in Moses' hand, when he came down from the mount, that Moses wist not that the ***skin of his face shone*** while he talked with Him. And when Aaron and all the children of Israel saw Moses, behold, the skin of his face shone; and they were afraid to come nigh him." (Exodus 34:29-30).

There is no short cut to passionate praying. Prayer is work! Hard work! Prayer will extract blood, as it were, from you. I have been in prayer meetings, where I have seen, heard, and experienced God's presence, and attempted to run away because of the awesomeness of His presence but the reigns of intercession would not let me go. I have had experiences where I have prayed until I felt like I was giving birth. This is when tears turn into groaning which cannot be uttered. It is at those times that I would become introspective, and transparent through the eyes of the Spirit, when all you want is to mortify the deeds of the flesh, and allow the will of God to spring forth out of the recesses of your soul. Under such intense prayer, a spirit of repentance takes a hold of you and you will be compelled to make it right with anyone you have wronged, and or you will feel the need to forgive those who have hurt you to the core.

Pride flees under intense prayer. In fact, the works of the flesh, of which pride is a part, cannot dwell in the life of a person who is given to passionate and intense prayers. The result of a life of prayer is the birthing of the fruit and gifts of Spirit. Prayer with heart-felt passion, will give you peace beyond human comprehension, and will mold and make you into a different person.

I can remember vividly, as a new convert, how I went after God with such intensity in prayer that my friends and neighbors would comment on hearing me pray. Then my neighbor who was like a mom to me, had a son, who before I got saved treated me as a sister. The devil got into him and he developed a hatred for me, it was scary. The enemy turned him against me with a vengeance. He banned me from visiting their home, even though his mom did not sanction his behavior. His cousin and I became Christians at the same time so we hung together. One day I was in her room and he surprised us by coming home early from work. He stormed in her room and he literally threw me out of his mother's house, hit me and threatened if he ever caught me there again it would be ugly, to put it mildly. This bullying continued for quite some time. On another occasion, we were walking home from Sunday night church service, in Jamaica, of course, and it was quite dark. Without any warning, he strung from nowhere with a piece of stick in his hand and started to hit, curse and threaten me. I was spared much harm because others were with me and warded him off. That experience was scary to say the least, but I kept praying and fasting for the Lord to help me through this trial. At first it was very hard for me to forgive or even pray for this guy. I wanted God to zap him (smile) but it did not happen. But through much prayer I was able to forgive him. After migrating to the United States, several years later, I decided to visit home. At this time his mom had passed away. He eventually lost his job, and lost a considerable amount of weight. (He went from an almost 300 pounder to a "Jack Sprat.") This same guy who threw me out of his mother's house, humbled himself, and spoke to me as though I was the Queen from Sheba, and guess what – he accepted my invitation to church. The remarkable thing was I felt such compassion for him that I never even thought of the wrong he had done to me; all I wanted was to see him saved and changed. Don't tell me prayer doesn't work. I tell you, you are a day late and a dime short.

Praying with passion will enable you to love your enemy, and to do good to those who despitefully use and abuse you. In order to reach into God' presence, one must be willing to lay all on the altar of sacrifice at the expense of the flesh being dissatisfied, and for the good of seeing God do wonders in and through the lives of others.

Another important aspect in seeking God is your posture before him. Always remember God is Sovereign and you are human. Therefore, reverential fear should be in order at the highest level when coming before him. Kneeling, bowing, and prostrating are definitely trademarks of those who understand the sovereignty and lordship of the Lord Jesus Christ. The key behind posturing is a heart of humility and respect for the Creator of the ends of the earth. King Ahab did wickedly before the Lord. He was positioned to be destroyed in 1 Kings 21:27, but note how he behaved when faced with his demise...*And it came to pass, when Ahab heard those words, that he rent his*

26

clothes, and put sackcloth upon his flesh, and fasted, and lay in sackcloth, and went softly. And the word of the Lord came to Elijah the Tishbite, saying, Seest thou how Ahab humbleth himself before me? because he humbleth himself before me, I will not bring the evil in his days: but in his son's days will I bring the evil upon his house.

There are many scripture references that support the posture of praying people. *Kneeling*: Daniel prayed on his knees three times a day (Dan. 6:10), Stephen fell on his knees and prayed before he died as a martyr (Acts 7:60), and Peter knelt down before the corpse of Tabitha to pray for her before she came back to life (Acts 9:40). *Sitting*: A good example is King David, who "went in and sat before the Lord, and he said . . ." (2 Sam. 7:18, NASB). *Standing*: One of the most telling cases is found in 2 Chronicles 20. When Judah was confronting the possibility of military attack, Jehoshaphat invited the people to pray. He stood up in the assembly in the house of the Lord and prayed for liberation while the people were "standing before the Lord" (2 Chron. 20:13, NASB). *Prostrating*: "David therefore besought God for the child; and David fasted and went in and lay (prostrate) all night on the floor." (2 Samuel 12:16) When you become desperate enough for something you will make yourself uncomfortable until that desire is met.

Intercessory Prayer

If you have ever experienced intercessory prayers, you will soon find that you need much energy, strength, and staying power to prevail in prayer, because leaving the earthly and getting into the heavenly, or the spirit world, will take the Holy Ghost and ministering angels to do battle with and for you. A person, who intends to pray serious prayers, must be prepared to fight against the principalities and powers of the devil. Daniel was a perfect example of fighting both earthly and heavenly

27

principalities and powers. But he won through much prayer! His earthly spiritual fights came from the men he worked with, and his heavenly battles came when satan realized God caught on to Daniels prayers. Satan commissioned legions of demons to stop Daniel's prayers, and it would have almost succeeded if the Lord did not send warring angels, namely Michael and Gabriel, to escort the answer back to Daniel. See Daniel 10. (I would strongly suggest that all who will dare to tread the waters of intercessory prayers, study the life of Daniel, not so much his prophecies, but his relationship with his God, and see if you still want the life of an intercessor.)

Satan is not annoyed when one prays simple marginal prayers because they have no effect or affect on his domain – the air. Remember in our ungodly state satan was the prince of the power of our domain. *Wherein in time past ye walked according to the course of this world, according to the prince of the **power of the air**, the spirit that now worketh in the children of disobedience.* (Eph 2:2) I looked at the Greek word for *air* in context to Eph. 2:2. Air means: psucho (*psoo'-kho) to breathe* (*voluntarily* but *gently*; thus differing on the one hand from, pneo (pneh-o) which denotes properly a *forcible* respiration; and on the other from the base of aer (*ah-ayr'*), which refers properly to an inanimate *breeze*), that is, (by implication of reduction of temperature by evaporation) to *chill* (figuratively): - wax cold.

I am not a theologian by any stretch of the imagination, but my limited understanding coupled with the infinite mind of Christ, I would say that the "air" that devil is prince of is ice/wax cold. Not so much that physical place Antarctica, but spiritually speaking to Antarctica. People who are under attack by the enemy, or who are possessed by the devil will experience some emotions that they describe as being cold or distant. The scriptures bear this out: *And the love of the great body of people*

28

will grow cold because of the multiplied lawlessness and iniquity, but he who endures to the end will be saved. (Matthew 12:12-13 Amplified) There is no warmth that comes from the dethroned prince of the power of the air.

No wonder the bible speaks of the devil being the unclean spirit in both Matt. 12:43 and Luke 11:24 which reads: *When the unclean spirit is gone out of a man, he walketh through dry places, seeking rest, and findeth none.* Dry in the Greek word Anudros (*an'-oo-dros*) means *waterless*, that is, *dry:* - dry, without water. The devil is living right now in a cold and dry place. Where the devil resides is so cold one could get frostbitten within seconds of exposure. We have heard the saying, the cold hands of death. Well the enemy is bloodless, yea lifeless, and like a parasitic leech he is seeking to suck you dry spiritually. Solomon said in Prov. 30 15-16...*There are three things that are never satisfied, yea, four things say not, It is enough:* ___**The grave;**___ *and the barren womb; the earth that is not filled with water; and the fire that saith not, It is enough.* The grave is a place where the devil does most of his dirty work. It is ever cold, clammy and unwelcoming.

I have a weapon for you prayer warrior or aspiring intercessor. When the devil comes close and you feel oppressed, cold and withdrawn, plead the BLOOD of Jesus Christ over your mind, thought pattern and body, repeatedly. Continue this regimen just like you would follow a doctor's order when prescribed antibiotics. The best result is seen when you take the prescribed dosage. Same is true with applying and pleading the blood of Jesus over your life. Stay at it until you get the victory. Rebuke the devil in Jesus' name just as the Lord did...*Resist the devil [stand firm against him], and he will flee from you.* (James 4:7 Amplified)

Prayer warriors, we need to be equipped with the knowledge of the word *"lest Satan should get an advantage of us: for we are not ignorant of his devices."* Be advised that the devil can only stay in dry places where no water is unless you let him in. In 1Peter 5:8-10, Peter mentioned that the devil is likened to a roaring lion, *(he is not a lion)*, seeking whom he may deceive or devour. Peter admonishes us to resist him, and that resistance can come in the form of aggressively praying or speaking the Word. You will suffer wounds due to resistance, but Peter said in the end...*the God of all grace, who hath called us unto his eternal glory by Christ Jesus, after that ye have suffered a while, make you perfect, stablish, strengthen, settle you.*

Speaking of resistance, I recall having a supervisor who was rather condescending at times. She would find fault with everything I did. She would let it be known that she was a part of a New Age Movement. She knew I was a Christian and I would let her know that I was praying for her. I meant it. I prayed for her salvation and for behavior modification to occur in her life. I was very cordial to her. Then one Monday morning after our small talk she said something to this effect, *"By the way, I was told by my leader to tell you to stop praying for me, because it was hindering the things that they were trying to accomplish."* My thought was "W*hat!*" You know when the devil sends you such a message it is like pouring fuel on fire. My prayers became more intense, and the trials became more severe, but I persisted and resisted the works of the devil. One day she got so mad at me for a minor issue which was not even a part of my duties. Long and short of it, she accused me of wanting her job, and the truth was it never even entered my thoughts concerning her job. During that time, our department was downsized, and of the four of us who worked in that department, I was the only one kept.

30

She was demoted to her previous role, and the others were reassigned. By no means am I glorying in the reassignment issue. There is indeed a higher level of spiritual thinking here. May I tell you, resistance begets resistance! The key here is you need God on your side. If not, the enemy of your soul will swallow you up and render you helpless and left for dead, but for the grace of Almighty God.

Like in the story of the three little pigs and the big bad wolf, the devil is seeking entrance into your home. I want to encourage you to build your spiritual house with the bricks and mortar of fasting and prayer. The two little pigs, using straws and sticks could not weather the storm of the big bad wolf; but like the little pig that built his house with bricks, when the wolf tried to blow his house in he failed miserably. Likewise, the devil will try to blow your house in, but with much prayer and fasting you must resist him, and do not allow him to get any warmth by your fire, because his coldness will put yours out, and you will be left out in the cold just like him. Let us bind ourselves together and like a mighty army push back satan and his agents to the coldest part of spiritual Antarctica. Now that is what you call hell!

Let us get back to the subject of praying passionate prayers. If you have never been there, be warned that the circumstances of life will push you into an active and intense passion in prayer. Examples of such prayers could come in any of the following forms, let's examine a few situations:

- When the doctors tell you your child has a few days to live, you will demonstrate passion in prayer.
- When you are told that your daughter was raped and murdered maliciously, then passion will come. Today we have Meghan's law because a parent was impassioned enough against a heartless criminal, to lobby government to

enact laws so others may not suffer as much as that parent did.

- When your spouse whom you love walked out because of infidelity, then you will get impassioned in prayer.
- When sexual immortality and debauchery of every kind grip your family or friends, then you will get impassioned in prayer.
- When the ministry or minister whom you trust becomes deceptive and forges ahead as though all is well, then you will become impassioned in prayer.
- When children are ruling parents; when government become robbers, thieves, promote and condone immoralities, and pass laws to justify their lack of conviction, just for the love and favor of a corrupt and wicked few, then you will get impassioned in prayer.
- When satan went up before God and demanded to sit on God's throne as it were, with no regard to whom he spoke, even God got impassioned and cast him out of heaven. (See Isaiah 14: 12-16)

I submit to you there will come a day in your life that an issue will get you so impassioned that you will even surprise yourself as to how aggressive and determined you will become in prayer.

Rizpah a Great Intercessor

I recall a bible character named Rizpah, when her sons were hanged because of the sin of their father Saul, how she refused to allow the birds of prey to eat her boys and those of Michal, Saul's daughter. Without any prompting, Rizpah laid sackcloth on a rock, and sat vigil over the dead bodies refusing to leave until her cause was heard. (Please note here that Michal had a surrogate who birthed her sons, so she did not react as passionately as Rizpah when her sons were ordered hanged. The bible did not mention Michal shedding a tear but we saw Rizpah's.) Incidentally, Rizpah name means "*a hot stone; also a tessellated pavement: - live coal, or pavement,* according to

32

Strong's Exhaustive Concordance. In other words, Rizpah was a hot baking stone, ready to resist any who threatened her heritage. No wonder the bible speaks of how the effectual fervent (*hot boiling*) prayer of the righteous avails much. (James 5:16) Rizpah stayed more than four months watching over her boys, through the process of decomposition, so that neither grave stealers nor preys would take her boys away. Her persistence, yea passion, caught the attention of King David, and he was forced into giving her boys a stately burial. (Read 2 Samuel 3:7 and 2 Samuel 21:8-14). *O, Lord, give us more Rizpah's with such passion to get our causes and issues heard, in Jesus' name. Amen!*

It was in August 2008, after ministering at a Mission's Conference in Brooklyn, New York, that I had one of the fieriest trials of my life. I remember after returning from the last night of services how the force of hell like never before issued an attack against my life. I never felt so sick in my life. I pushed through the feeling and went to my home church the following Sunday morning. After service, I was driving home, when a sudden dizzy and disorientating feeling came over me. I could hardly see the road in front of me. I could only pull over and call for help. A few sisters came to my rescue and I ended up in the nearest Hospital. My blood count was extremely low and the doctor had to give me a quick dose of Iron to get me on the right track, well so I thought. After a few hours of observation, I was not stabilized, so the doctor thought it best for me to stay overnight to make sure all was well. Hesitantly, I agreed...wrong decision, well so I thought, because God ultimately got the glory, and I got the victory.

The next day after a battery of tests, I noticed that I was getting increasingly weak and disoriented. They realized that I needed thyroid medication to stabilize my hormones. That was mistake number two. Instead of getting better I was getting worst. My sister and church family started a prayer vigil for me. I recall going in and out of consciousness and started to hallucinate. The doctors were now saying I was depressed and I needed some kind of psychiatric care. They were ready to prescribe psyche medications for me. The devil is a liar. The long and short of it is that I was being overdosed on Iron supplements, which was administered by the hospital.

Throughout the entire ordeal, I remembered the message I preached days before, *"The enemies you see today you will see them no more forever."* (I kept hearing that verse of scripture playing in my head like a broken record, and I held on to it for dear life.) These words came from Exodus 14:13… *And Moses said unto the people, Fear ye not, standstill, and see the salvation of the Lord, which he will shew to you today:* **_for the Egyptians whom ye have seen today, ye shall see them again no more forever._**

One of the days of my stay in the hospital, when I felt as if it was going to be my last on the planet, I took my bible, opened it, and placed it on my head, held it there. With tears in my eyes I asked God to allow His Word to seep into my spirit and soul. I wanted His words to seep in my soul like a wall that had cracks where water could penetrate. Call me crazy if you will, but who told Joshua to challenge God to tell the sun to stand still in the valley of Ajalon until he destroyed the enemy. I cried out with every ounce of strength I could muster to the God of Heaven and asked him to come to my rescue. And he did!

I remembered how the spirit of satan came in my hospital room and told me he was going to kill me. I cast my eyes upon him, like Paul did to Elymas the sorcerer in Acts 13: 10-11 *(And said, O full of all subtlety and all mischief, thou child of the devil, thou enemy of all righteousness, wilt thou not cease*

34

to pervert the right ways of the Lord? And now, behold, the hand of the Lord is upon thee, and thou shalt be blind, not seeing the sun for a season. And immediately there fell on him a mist and a darkness; and he went about seeking some to lead him by the hand.) I rebuked that evil spirit in the name of Jesus Christ. I told him I will not die but live to declare the works of the Lord. Immediately following that encounter, a spirit of intercessory prayer took a hold of me in the CCU (critical care unit). I told the devil *"you will not hurt me or any other patient in this hospital."* At this point, the nurses thought I was really going crazy but I knew where my strength rested. Thank God for the Holy Ghost and his guiding angels in the time of trouble. I now know and am assured that God Almighty does lead *through* the valley of the shadow of death.

I was told by my sister that during one of the nights when I was at my lowest point, (I can only remember that my bed was surrounded by prayer warriors), how they prayed. She told me that she never saw people interceding like that in all her life. She said one of the brothers; Bro. Calvin, doubled over on the ground, with intercessory groans, spoke in tongues and fought hell on my behalf. I am convinced today that if I was not an intercessor for others when I was able to, I would have been a victim of both medical malpractice, and spiritual assassination.

I want to thank the Lord for being on my side first of all, and for sending my prayer partners and fellow Christian sisters to stand up to the medical team and would not allow them to administer any psychiatric medicine to me; because they were able to discern the hand of the enemy at work and prayed me out of the jaws of death. Again, a big "Thank You" to all those who labored in prayer for me during this time of adversity. The Lord Jesus Christ will not forget your labor of love. I was eventually released from the hospital without any reference to psychiatric or psychological care. Thank you Jesus!

Let us pray. Father, in the name of Jesus, I thank you for your healing, protection and provision, and above all for the strength I have gained through intercessory prayer. Bless the readers of this book right now with the grace to endure during their time of tribulation. Let a spirit of intercession fall upon this reader at this time, and let there be a birthing of passion in the soul right now, in Jesus' name. Amen!

Insights and Prayer Points for Praying with Passion.

You must

1. Have a *"want to"* mentally, physically and spiritually to pray with passion. *As the hart, pants for the water brook so pants my soul for thee Oh God.(Psm. 42:1)*
2. Be willing to separate from certain friends and even family members (not preaching isolationism but be an adult in understanding) to consecrate yourself to the Lord. Hanging out with God must take precedence over others.
3. Set yourself free and allow the Holy Spirit to use you whenever He sees fit. In other words, surrender your will and purpose to His will and purpose.
4. Be ready to do battle with the:
    a. World - It will compete with your desires in areas like entertainment, fads, fashions, wealth etc. *Guard your heart with all diligence, for out of it are the issues of life.(Prov. 4:23)*
    b. Flesh – Fasting and prayer will become your ally not your enemy. The belly loves food, but you will soon see the Spirit will call for food out of the mouth of Lord.
    c. Devil – The tempter will show his ugly head. Be quick to recognize his devices and resist him forthwith with the Word of the Lord.
5. Be vigilant at *ALL* times. The serpent is on the prowl.
6. Put on and keep on the whole armor of God.
7. Possess the ability to cry genuine tears. They are not only needed it is required to supplicate before the Lord. If you have lost your tears, ask God to allow you to cry again. I lost my ability to cry once because some people would ridicule me when I worshipped and prayed because tears would wash my soul. I told God to take my tears away and make me be like everybody else. May I tell you that that was one of the worst prayers I ever prayed? It came to a point in my life that some of those

same people who used to criticize me started to notice my dry eyes. I had to go back and ask the Lord for pardon, and to tell the truth, sometime I still feel like my tears are not fully restored. A great way to have a soft heart is to become compassionate; it will melt the heart every time. Just a word of wisdom to our men. Real men do cry. Jesus not only cried, HE WEPT!

8. Live a repentant life. This is a sure way to keep the channels of righteousness open in your heart and soul. God draws near to a repentant heart and penitent spirit.

9. Be presumptuous on a positive level, of course. ***Pray willfully and avoid sin purposefully***. With that mentality, you will be attractive to God and His Holy angels.

10. Pray always. Jesus said men ought always to pray and not to faint. The key to praying is simple. Create and abide in a prayerful mind set. I am not saying that you should become a zombie, but on the contraire, maintain a healthy spiritual state of being. Eph. 5:19 puts it this way…*speaking to yourselves in psalms and hymns and spiritual songs, singing and making melody in your heart to the Lord.*

11. Meditate on his words constantly.

12. Maintain the Spirit of the Lord in your conversations.

13. Be sensitive to what I call *"holy nudges"* to pray for others. You would be surprised how the Lord will place others on your heart at specific times to pray for their needs and results usually occur, with or without your knowledge. By the way, you cannot pray for others without being blessed yourself. It is impossible. I believe this is one of the hidden blessings of praying unselfishly.

14. Applying the insights mentioned above will place you in a position to find your calling as a prayer warrior.

Psalms 142

1. I cried unto the Lord with my voice; with my voice unto the Lord did I make my supplication.

2. I poured out my complaint before him; I shewed before him my trouble.

3. When my spirit was overwhelmed within me, then thou knewest my path. In the way wherein I walked have they privily laid a snare for me.

4. I looked on my right hand, and beheld, but there was no man that would know me: refuge failed me; no man cared for my soul.

5. I cried unto thee, O Lord: I said, Thou art my refuge and my portion in the land of the living.

6. Attend unto my cry; for I am brought very low: deliver me from my persecutors; for they are stronger than I.

7. Bring my soul out of prison, that I may praise thy name: the righteous shall compass me about; for thou shalt deal bountifully with me.

Chapter Two

Second Principle

Openly Confess Your Convictions

For with the heart man believeth to righteousness; and with the mouth confession is made to salvation. Romans 10:10.

My prosperity is based upon two things: *HIS WILL* and *MY CONFESSIONS.* The Lord's will is that none should perish but that all should come to repentance. However, the Lord will not force anyone to serve Him, and He should not have to. He gave every man that inherent ability to choose. In one situation, the Lord speaking through Moses to the Israelites said, "*I call heaven and earth to record this day against you, that I have set before you life and death, blessing and cursing: **therefore choose life, that both thou and thy seed may live**.*" (Deu. 30:19) The Lord requires free will service, and rightfully so. You or I would not want anyone to serve us grudgingly or in a half hearted manner. We demand much more since we have the choice to take our business elsewhere. I believe the LORD, the Creator of the ends of earth deserves nothing but the best of service. Wouldn't you agree?

Open confession will lead to conviction. King Solomon said open rebuke is better than secret love. When David sinned against the Lord, the Lord spoke to His prophet Nathan to confront David. David's response of brokenness led him to confess his sins, as recorded in his famous psalm of repentance, Psalm 51, which we today can use as a blue print to get our deliverance. Careful observation showed that David truly repented. He said God would not despise one with a broken and contrite heart. David's restoration to God's favor rested on his confession. C. H. Spurgeon captures this concept of confession when he so eloquently states:

> With the mouth confession is made unto salvation. (Romans 10:10) There must be no confession with the mouth where there is not a believing heart. To profess a faith which you have not is to make yourself a deceptive trader who pretends to be carrying on a very large business, while he has no stock, no capital, and is only obtaining credit on false pretense, and so, is a thief. To make a profession, without having a possession, is to be a cloud without rain—a riverbed choked up with dry stones—utterly without water. It is to be a mere play-actor, strutting about for an hour with the name and garment of a king, to be exchanged, behind the scenes, for the garb of poverty and the character of shame.

So, why is confession the life-blood of our Christian existence? It is God's designed. *Confess your sins to each other and pray for each other so that you may be healed. The earnest prayer of a righteous person has great power and produces wonderful results.* (James 5:16 NLT). Here are five reasons why we should use confession in our walk with the Lord and also in our prayers:

1. It is scriptural, and not a random collection of human ingenuity. *"All Scripture is God-breathed and is useful for teaching, rebuking, correcting and training in righteousness, so that the man of God may be thoroughly equipped for every good work."* (2 Timothy 3:16-17 NSAB)
2. We are fallible, prone to errors, and short on godly principles. *"Because sentence against an evil work is not executed speedily, therefore the heart of the sons of men is fully set in them to do evil"*--Eccl. 8:11.
3. It is impossible to please the Lord without faith, which is the stabilizer of our spiritual existence. Heb. 11:6 states, *"but without faith it is impossible to please him: for he that cometh to God must believe that he is, and that he is a rewarder of them that diligently seek him."*
4. We are an evangelical people. We have a mandate from the Lord to reach all men before the great and notable day of the Lord comes...*Go into all the world and preach the Good News to everyone.* (Mark 16:15 (NLT))
5. We need a guide, compass and direction to our ultimate destination—heaven, to be with our precious Lord and Savior, Jesus Christ. *How can a young man keep his way pure? By living according to your word.* (Psm. 119:9 NIV)

Sincere confession will lead us into a more open and deeper relationship with the Lord. The Apostle Luke in Acts 3:19 spoke of the refreshing that comes only from the presence of the Lord, and it is contingent upon us to have a repentant heart and a converted soul, which equates to a transparent life before Him.

Let me share a practical principle that I learnt in my early years of professional development as a Corporate Trainer. I was introduced to a prolific author speaker and trainer, Brian Tracey. He gave a seminar on developing your best self for making public presentations or delivering a speech in general.

He used a seemingly ridiculous technique that he said would drive your fears away or at least push it into the background, and accentuate your self-confidence. He said, before you make a presentation, find a mirror, square your shoulder, look straight into your own eyes and say, "I like myself!" He said you will feel utterly ridiculous at first, but keep saying it. If you keep saying it, he said, you will begin to laugh at yourself for that crazy exercise, but after several tries, you will see your self-confidence increase, and you will also see that your audience will start to say I like this guy or gal as well. Try it. I did and still do this exercise if I become overwhelmed when I have to make a public speech. Why was it necessary to share that piece with you? It is simple. I want to let you know that you *must have* and *must confess* positive declarations and affirmations about yourself before you can truly validate others. Jesus said you must love *your neighbor* as *yourself.* I submit to you that you cannot give what you do not possess. As of today, start confessing what you want in your life. Your speech will determine your destiny. Solomon was dubbed the wisest man because of his views on life. He said, "*A man hath joy (delight, bliss, elation, ecstasy... etc.) by the answer (response) of his mouth (speech): a word spoken in due season, how good is it! A word fitly spoken (in the right season) is like apples of gold in pictures of silver.*" (Proverbs 15:23 & 25:11). Speak and pray in present tense about yourself, even if whatever you spoke or prayed about seems to be a zillion miles away from your current reality. You will notice after a while that you and that great divide will meet and become great friends. Somebody shout, "I like myself. I am successful. I am a Prayer Warrior, in Jesus' name!" Shout, "I love my God!" I felt that, O Glory!

Let's examine one of the many stories told about the Patriarch Abraham, the request to sacrifice his son Isaac.

Abraham was faced with one of the most challenging trials of his life, as recorded in Genesis 22, as he obeyed God's command to take his son, his only son Isaac to Mount Moriah to offer him up as a free will offering to the Lord. Abraham had an inner confession and belief that he and his son *would return* after the sacrifice. With such a confession, Abraham's faith moved God to provide a ram for the sacrifice. He received joy by the response of his mouth and heart.

An old preacher once said, *"Jehovah will always Jireh."* The LORD will always provide. I like that! I want to mirror the things that the mighty men and women of God did and said, and how the Lord responded to their positive declarations. I am crazy enough to believe if God did it for them he will certainly do it for me. Did not the word of God say that *the scriptures were given for an example for us to follow?* Think about it. Let's adopt this principle of open confessions of our convictions. Let's practice it in our speech, our prayers, and in our daily lives, and watch God work for us, and above all, take note on how your outlook on life and spiritual things change for the better.

In my walk with the Lord, I have come to realized that my confessions have truly changed my perception on life itself. Also, "the issues" that usually accompany life seem to get smaller now since I have changed the way I see, speak and pray about things. I have banked my confidence in this verse of scripture: *Death and life are in the power of the tongue: and they that love it shall eat the fruit thereof.* (Proverbs 18:21) Walk in liberty, for whom the Son sets free is free indeed.

Let me share two quick stories with you that I feel will solidify my stance of speaking positively, and hopefully they will rekindle some fire in you. I am currently an Adjunct Professor at a senior and junior college respectively. One course that I teach at the senior college at the graduate level is

Motivational Leadership. I would open the course with this scripture; **Death and life are in the power of the tongue.** I tell my students that before we proceed into the study they must change their paradigm about the course itself and its outcome. I would then inform them that they have already been graded as an "A" student. If they receive any other grade, it is because they chose that grade. After other preliminaries, I would have them quote the scripture; and, this drill would be done intermittently during the course. Invariably there would be times when the spirit of negativism reared its ugly head, and we would quote that scripture again. It came to the point where the students themselves began to quote the scripture to ward off any negativism. The final course work required a research paper. Several students quoted Proverbs 21:18 to anchor their position as a strong motivational leader. Believe me as I relate this story, at the end of each class, all of the students who bought into the concept of speaking positively received an "A" as a passing grade. I remember this one particular class, as I was doing my farewells, they asked me to take a seat because they also wanted to speak into my life as I had spoken into their lives. They told me that they were sure I was *"sent"* to teach them. They went on to say that they knew that I was called to minister, and that I should not do anything else, because it was evident, the Lord's hand was on my life. (*This is secular college we are talking about here, my friends.*) I usually let my class know in an icebreaker form that I consider myself a *"princess"* since my Father is King, and if they wanted any favors, they should know how to address me. (*This tactic usually genders some laughter, and creates a sense of normalcy.*) Well, it registered. The group said not only was I a *"princess for the Lord"* but I had become *"their princess."* They proceeded to take out a tiara from a beautiful gift bag, and crowned me in front of the entire class.

They charged me not to take it off until I got home. I was shocked to say the least. After the initial shock wore off, I was beside myself. I screamed and shouted, Thank You Jesus! Hallelujah! Glory to God! I was going crazy to say the least. They just cheered me on. And guess what, I strolled through the campus with my tiara and gave the princess wave too, no, I did not wave, but wanted to though. I tell you there is no better feelings than having your students validate you. There is nothing like it. Nothing! O for the power of openly confessing your convictions! I dare you to try it!

In another case at the junior college, I was teaching a customer service class to people who were victims of the recession. To put a positive spin on the situation, I preempted my class by using the same scripture, and they were asked to quote it. I told them that we would only confess and accentuate the positive and eliminate the negative. I had 21 students, all except four, who were over the age of 30. During the course I would interject positive quotations, and openly confess my convictions about who the head of my life is, and how I would not be successful if it had not been the Lord who was on my side. I must mention that through all of this, I had not worked full time since January 2008. Even with that reality, I refused to make it an issue, because I strongly believe that my confessions will determine my destiny.

So, one day, this student, a nice little lady came to me after class, and just poured out her heart to me. And trust me it had nothing to do with the course work. I listened and offered to say a prayer for her. She agreed and I did pray. She went on to ask about my church affiliation and I shared that with her as well. It so happened that I was asked to be the keynote speaker at a Prayer Breakfast at a church near her home in Queens, NY. So I took the opportunity to invite her and she came. One of the texts for the message I presented was, yes, you guessed right, Proverbs 18:21 ***Death and life are in the power of the tongue: and they that love it shall eat the fruit thereof.*** The Holy Spirit ministered that morning. When I was through ministering, my student came to the altar, repented of her sins, received the baptism of the Holy Ghost with the evidence of speaking with another tongues, and was baptized in the wonderful name of Jesus Christ. Now this is what you would call a "Prayer Breakfast." Lord I thank you for your manifold blessings on us.

What if I had just shared the classic customer service philosophy? This soul would have never experienced such life changing encounter. Might I add, I never begin a class without seeking the Lord and asking Him to make me a blessing to at least one soul. I know I must do my duties as a faithful employee, but guess what? I am not divided from my call. I am a Christian first and foremost, and my job is a means to an end, not an end in and of itself. When I cannot help someone spiritually at my place of employment, I declare to you, my purpose there is over, and I start asking the Lord for new assignments. Could it be that I was laid off from full time work to meet the need of this soul in Queens, NY? Only eternity will tell, but for now, I believe strongly it was. *Thank you Jesus for saving my soul, and allowing me the privilege to serve in our kingdom!*

I want to encourage you right now to be a sharer. Share your testimony with others. You never know how your life story might change someone's life and its direction. Pray about it. That is how I approach all my engagements. Just do it. Pray in Jesus' name. I see you squirming in your seat saying I do not know about that. *Hey, you, yes, you. You can do this, go for it. The Lord and I believe in you.*

After sharing those true stories with you, I am even more resolute about my confessions and convictions. I dare say if I confess doom and gloom that is what I will have and possess. On the other hand, if I confess the things that are life giving and generative then I will get what is life giving and generative.

My speech does determine my destiny. Likewise, how and what I pray for will have a profound impact on my destiny as well. With that foreknowledge, I will only speak and pray the things God and I want to see fulfilled in my life. These are some of my personal confessions. Some might think that I am too audacious in my affirmation, but I dare say I cannot have the things I want from God, or do the things I want to do for God with whimsical and tentative confessions. Carl Von Clausewitz, (July 1, 1780 – November 16, 1831) was a Prussian soldier, military historian and military theorist. He said, "Make your choice, therefore, according to this inner force; but never forget that no military leader has ever become great without audacity." Paul calls it "NOW FAITH!" So what I speak NOW will happen in my future be it negative or positive. Therefore, I will speak only positive things in my life NOW, in Jesus' name. Here goes! I am who God says I am. I am fearfully and wonderfully made. I am full of the Holy Ghost. I will stay under God's faucet until He chooses to do otherwise with me. I have all nine fruit of the spirit residing and operating in me. I release all the virtues of love, joy, peace, long suffering, gentleness, goodness, faith, meekness, and temperance, in my spirit and life. I am open to be used by God in any or in all of the nine gifts of the spirit. I covet the gifts that the Lord knows are best for me. My body is the temple of the Holy Ghost, so I will guard it with all kinds of prayer and fasting. I will sing my best songs unto the LORD. I will make melody in my heart and my lips shall sing aloud all His praises. When I pray the prayer of Faith, whatever I call forth shall come to pass in Jesus' name. When I lay hands on the sick, they shall recover in Jesus' name. I am for the LORD and His cause;

therefore, I am against all things that He is against. I am open to His leading, so speak my Lord. The Lord has the helicopter view, so He knows which way to take. I will submit my will to His. Life will throw both hits and misses, but *by George* I will not stop swinging, odds are I will hit more home runs than not. These are a few of my confessions. What are you waiting on, start listing yours _NOW_ in Jesus name!

King Solomon shared some of my passion when he declared *"I will not be afraid of sudden fear, neither of the desolation of the wicked, when it cometh. For the LORD shall be my confidence, and shall keep thy foot from being taken. I will also lay me down to sleep without fear; When thou liest down, thou shalt not be afraid: yea, thou shalt lie down, and thy sleep shall be sweet."(*Prov. 3:25-26) I, therefore, confess my dreams are focused and directed on the things that are productive and forward thinking. When the dream stealers surface the angel of the Lord will destroy them. I will fight my best fight but will know when to dispatch angels to do wars and battles on my behalf. Angels are there as ministers to those who are the heirs of salvation. They are commissioned to stay with me and you for life. *"The angel of the Lord encampeth round about them that fear him, and delivereth them. Surely goodness and mercy shall follow me all the days of my life: and I will dwell in the house of the Lord forever."* (Psalms 34:7 & 23:6)

Where the humanist and other self absorbed observers go wrong, is not realizing that the breath that we breathe comes from the One who spoke all things into existence, and all, bar none, have a part of God's DNA (genetic material) running up and down in our veins and psyche. God said, Let there be. He did not say this only to the just, but to all men who have his genes. This idea to look to "the self" for the answer as opposed to looking to "the One" who gave the cognitive ability to even seek an answer is not plausible. Dear Lord, please *open our eyes because we are indeed sleeping the sleep of death* as stated in Psalms 13:3.

Openness is another key component of getting your victory through prayer. The Lord, through the psalmist, echoed these words, *"I [am] the LORD thy God who brought thee out of the land of Egypt: open thy mouth wide, and I will fill it."* Psalm 81:10. Paul chimed in, *"For with the heart man believeth unto righteousness; and with **the mouth confession** is made unto salvation."* Romans 10:10. Solomon went on to say in Proverbs 15:23. *A man hath **joy by the answer of his mouth**: and a word [spoken] in due season, how good [it is]!* Isaiah 46:10 states *"Declaring the end from the beginning, and from ancient times the things that are not yet done, saying, My counsel shall stand, and I will do all my pleasure:"* And Job anchors it by declaring, *"Thou shalt also decree a thing, and it shall be established unto thee."* *(Job* 22:27) You must state your conviction openly about your intentions to serve and please God, as well as where you see yourself now and in the future. These confessions will not come naturally, but through much prayer, training and retraining of your mind and tongue to be in obedience to the will and word of God.

Someone said *keep your eyes out of the rear view mirror.* If you do keep your focus on the rear view, odds are, you are going to crash. It is the words you confessed in your past that will one day save or sever your life in the future. Choose your words wisely. Shakespeare had great insight when he said, *"This above all to thine own self be true, and it must follow, as the night the day, thou canst not then be false to any man."* King David was known for many things, his fight and victory over Goliath of Gath, his crazy worship, his generosity to the kingdom to build a house for the Lord, and his warrior-ship and leadership traits. But when faced with vengeance he said concerning Saul his enemy, *"The Lord forbid that I should do this thing unto my master, the Lord's anointed, to stretch forth mine hand against him, seeing he is the anointed of the Lord."* (1 Samuel 24: 6). I must add that David had an insight into the spiritual world that must not be underestimated. Even though Saul was the person pursuing his life to take it, he also knew that Saul was possessed with the spirit of darkness, and only he, David, was given the key of music to calm Saul's demons. Let's ask the Lord to grant us discernment of spirits, with proper application for living.

David was the all time Jewish boy. But, what caught my attention was David's brutal honesty with his God. David wanted nothing more than to please his God. When he sinned, he was so remorseful and penitent that God had to listen and show mercy on him. David's prayer of repentance in Psalm 51:1 is my all time favorite. *Have mercy upon me, O God, according to thy loving-kindness: according unto the multitude of thy tender mercies blot out my transgressions.* David used words that were action oriented and demonstrated accountability and responsibility. He was not tentative and did not use rhetoric to cover his behavior. Using words like *have mercy on me, wash me, I acknowledge my sin, purge me, create in me, restore unto me, deliver me...etc.,* then he said *I will teach transgressors thy ways and sinner shall be converted to thee.* David was one of the first to give back in community service as it were. In essence he was saying I went through this shame and reproach because of my behavior and I will, if at all possible, bar the door with my confessions to say don't go where I went in sin because ...***but the way of transgressors is hard.*** *(Proverbs 13:15)*

David wore his heart not just on his sleeves, but David cast himself on the mercies of the Lord. Can you image how

David felt when he openly confessed his wrong and made it right to his God? I know how suffocating and uncomfortable it feels when I sin against the Lord. When you break the law of the land there is that nervousness that you feel on the inside that would make you do some insane things.

May I encourage you, if you can relate to David's life, do not stop your fight to confess, forsake and turn from your wicked ways, as stated. 2 Chronicles 7:14 One of these days, salvation is going to come to your house, and no devil in hell will be able to laugh or point his crooked finger of condemnation in your face, ever again.

Paul to the Romans recalls his human frailty and confessed, in Rom.7:15 *For that which I do I allow not: for what I would, that do I not;* ***but what I hate, that do I***. He also cried out in verse 7:24...*O wretched man that I am! who shall deliver me from the body of this death?* But, thanks be to God who never leaves us without a way of escape. Romans 8 verse 1 states... ***There is therefore now no condemnation to them which are in Christ Jesus, who walk not after the flesh, but after the Spirit.*** When you openly confess your sins to the Lord, it takes the guilt and pain away. A sense of freedom fills your heart and you literally feel liberated. There is nothing like the power of openness in repentance, NOTHING like it! ***Thank you Father for forgiving us our sins; O, how we love and appreciate you for it. Thank you Jesus!***

Insights and Prayer Points for Praying with Openness

1. Be honest with yourself, your God, and your neighbor.
2. Confession and humility goes hand in hand. Be quick to make things right, your breakthrough depends on it. Let it become a lifestyle.
3. Identify you. Get to know you. Be you. Do not spend your energy trying to be someone else other than Jesus Christ: By the way, you will see His traits in the godly, emulate the traits but remain you.
4. Be transparent to God and ultimately others will come to trust you. Figuratively speaking, take all the locks off the doors in your life and give Jesus Christ full access, you will soon see that He will remain a resident. Since you have given Him free access, allow him to rearrange your priorities. I guarantee that you will not be disappointed with his redesign strategy.
5. David said search me O God and know my heart. See if there is any wicked way in me. Allow the Holy Spirit to have full control of your life. Solomon in Proverbs 20:27 said, *The spirit of man is the candle of the LORD, searching all the inward parts of the belly.* The Lord will use your own spirit to search out your own intentions and motivations. You cannot lie to two persons, yourself and the Lord, so simply submit and allow the Lord to make you into who he wants you to be. Jesus said to Saul, *"it is hard for thee to kick against the pricks."*
6. Relax and permit the Lord to lead you into the plain paths of His righteousness. I submit to you that you will be able to see some things only reserved to those who will permit the Lord to lead.

Psalms 143

1. *Hear my prayer, O Lord, give ear to my supplications: in thy faithfulness answer me, and in thy righteousness.*
2. *And enter not into judgment with thy servant: for in thy sight shall no man living be justified.*
3. *For the enemy hath persecuted my soul; he hath smitten my life down to the ground; he hath made me to dwell in darkness, as those that have been long dead.*
4. *Therefore is my spirit overwhelmed within me; my heart within me is desolate.*
5. *I remember the days of old; I meditate on all thy works; I muse on the work of thy hands.*
6. *I stretch forth my hands unto thee: my soul thirsteth after thee, as a thirsty land. Selah.*
7. *Hear me speedily, O Lord: my spirit faileth: hide not thy face from me, lest I be like unto them that go down into the pit.*
8. *Cause me to hear thy lovingkindness in the morning; for in thee do I trust: cause me to know the way wherein I should walk; for I lift up my soul unto thee.*
9. *Deliver me, O Lord, from mine enemies: I flee unto thee to hide me.*
10. *Teach me to do thy will; for thou art my God: thy spirit is good; lead me into the land of uprightness.*
11. *Quicken me, O Lord, for thy name's sake: for thy righteousness' sake bring my soul out of trouble.*
12. *And of thy mercy cut off mine enemies, and destroy all them that afflict my soul: for I am thy servant.*

Chapter Three

Third Principle

Work the WORD

Thy word is a lamp unto my feet, and a light unto my path. Psalm 119:105.

On July 24, 2009 I woke to a text message from my sister Karen. She wrote, *"Did you know the Lord can turn your life upside down in a second?"* My first reaction was what went wrong. So I called and asked quizzically what happened? She heard the concern in my voice and said, "What's wrong? Girl, the Lord just spoke a word into my spirit and I am holding onto it." So, I said so cavalierly it only takes a Word from the Lord. She got so excited. She said, "That's it – a WORD from the Lord, that's all it takes."

It is so amazing how it only takes *one* WORD from the Lord in a split second that can facilitate a paradigm shift in your life. The Lord promised never to give you more than you can bear. In Exodus 12: 40-41 says *Now the sojourning of the children of Israel, who dwelt in Egypt, was four hundred and thirty years. And it came to pass at the end of the four hundred and thirty years, even the selfsame day it came to pass, that all the hosts of the Lord went out from the land of Egypt.* I want to highlight this portion of the scripture that said...*four hundred and thirty years, even the selfsame day it came to pass*...the selfsame day tells me that when your trial, or tribulation comes to an end, or is declared over, and your file as it were is sealed, the prosecutor has to close his case too. He, the prosecutor, or I dare say, the enemy, cannot change or alter that final decision set forth on your behalf. Listen, I am ready, with bags packed, to get out of the situation that the enemy told me would never end. When God declares and decrees it to be over, then it is OVER! It took a word of hatred to sell Joseph in bondage, but it took a Word from the Lord to pull him out. Prophetically, it took over 20 years for Joseph's dream to be fulfilled, but when it came to pass, Joseph walked out of prison in style. I liked how David, in Psalm 105:17-22, summarized the sequence of events:

1. Pharaoh, the king, sent a word to him
2. it loosed his shackles
3. it set him free
4. it made him a wise ruler over the kings house, substance and princes, and
5. allowed Israel's exodus story to be told even today.

What a WORD! What a GOD! I felt I needed to share the end of Joseph's story before I reviewed his dilemma. Joseph was a happy-go-lucky child. He knew he was daddy's boy and he would not let his brothers forget it. After many years of sibling rivalry on the part of his brothers, they planned and executed a brother's worst nightmare. Joseph was sold to slave traders, with no hope of ever seeing his family again. Joseph was now separated from all he knew to be familiar and was at the mercy of total strangers for a measly price of twenty pieces of silver. Joseph was banished to a place that was never a part of his many dreams or his own destiny.

Joseph had his father's heart. He was the son of Jacob's favorite wife. He no doubt resembled his mother, and every time Jacob saw Joseph he saw Rachel. Jacob promised he would make Rachel proud if she was around. As Jacob reminisced, and even planned Joseph's future, he would share it with his elder sons. His sons grew increasingly weary of their father talking of how Joseph was his prized possession. No doubt, they hypocritically nodded and even gave suggestions on how he would be prosperous, yet in their hearts, they only had hatred and malice for their younger brother.

In the process of time hatred was almost transformed into murder had it not been for the Lord's hand upon Joseph. His brothers conjured up a scheme of deception that fooled their father for over twenty years. One would wonder where Joseph got this conviction when his brothers exuded such deceptive behaviors.

I do not know when it all happened but one day Joseph got up and decided I am going to practice the principles of my father. He would remember the days when his father Jacob would pray to this invisible God – Jehovah by name. He reminisced of family gatherings, and how Jacob would tell of the promises of Jehovah God. He remembered how his dad mentioned how God would one day give them a land flowing with milk and honey, where they will never have to be nomadic anymore. For just one moment in time Joseph saw in his mind' eye, a place of tranquility. But those thoughts would abruptly disappear when Joseph was summoned to serve his captors.

For some reason though, Joseph had in his mind that one day his deliverance would come. David in the Psalms 126 reminded us that the Lord would one day turn again his captivity. Why, would you ask that I spent so much time rehearsing the life of Joseph? It is because I am rehearsing the WORD. The only way you will have power in prayer is to know and declare the word of the Lord. Jesus, being very God, used the word of God consistently. He (Jesus) is famous for saying…*it is written*. If

Jesus who had all power returned to the Word for weaponry against the enemy, how much more should we as saints of God apply the Word of God to our daily lives, and above all, in our time of prayer.

I have learned that reading the word of God during prayer is one of the most effective tools in defeating the plan of the devil. I have used the Word when I cannot find my own words to pray. The secret though to this principle of praying The Word is to take the BIBLE along with you in your time of prayer and meditation. Take a few seconds to meditate on this passage of scripture and see how you could incorporate this in your prayer time and feel the effects of praying the WORD.

> *Deal with thy servant according unto thy mercy, and teach me thy statutes. I am thy servant; give me understanding, that I may know thy testimonies. It is time for thee, Lord, to work: for they have made void thy law. Therefore I love thy commandments above gold; yea, above fine gold. Therefore I esteem all thy precepts concerning all things to be right; and I hate every false way. Thy testimonies are wonderful: therefore doth my soul keep them. The entrance of thy words giveth light; it giveth understanding unto the simple. I opened my mouth, and panted: for I longed for thy commandments. Look thou upon me, and be merciful unto me, as thou usest to do unto those that love thy name. Order my steps in thy word: and let not any iniquity have dominion over me. (Psm. 119:124-133)*

There is such a sweet aroma of the presence of the Lord that comes from his Word into our hearts that no human thinking can comprehend. I love His Word. In the same passage you just read, it says, *"The entrance of your words giveth light."* I feel impressed by the Holy Spirit as I am penning this paragraph to insert another psalm for your mediation. I would not mind if you simply stop reading my words and allow His words to have its perfect work in your life.

The heavens declare the glory of God; and the firmament sheweth his handywork. Day unto day uttereth speech, and night unto night sheweth knowledge. There is no speech nor language, where their voice is not heard. Their line is gone out through all the earth, and their words to the end of the world. In them hath he set a tabernacle for the sun, which is as a bridegroom coming out of his chamber, and rejoiceth as a strong man to run a race. His going forth is from the end of the heaven, and his circuit unto the ends of it: and there is nothing hid from the heat thereof. The law of the Lord is perfect, converting the soul: the testimony of the Lord is sure, making wise the simple. The statutes of the Lord are right, rejoicing the heart: the commandment of the Lord is pure, enlightening the eyes. The fear of the Lord is clean, enduring for ever: the judgments of the Lord are true and righteous altogether. More to be desired are they than gold, yea, than much fine gold: sweeter also than honey and the honeycomb. Moreover by them is thy servant warned: and in keeping of them there is great reward. Who can understand his errors? cleanse thou me from secret faults. Keep back thy servant also from presumptuous sins; let them not have dominion over me: then shall I be upright, and I shall be innocent from the great transgression. Let the words of my mouth, and the meditation of my heart, be acceptable in thy sight, O Lord, my strength, and my redeemer.
(Psalms 19:1-14)

Let's pray, *Lord Jesus, your words are life giving. Breathe life in your child right now. Where there is hate bring love. Where there is pain, soothe. Minister strength to the hurting, strengthen the feeble knees. Encourage the discouraged and discontented. Bring peace to the troubled heart. Restore the things that are broken, which is the source of this pain right now. Bring home a wayward child. Convert the unconverted and bind up all their wounds. Peace Speaker, Holy Father, Precious Jesus, wrap your loving arms around your child and grant him/her peace in Jesus' name. AMEN!*

I remember attending one of our regular Saturday morning prayer service at my church. This particular Saturday I felt like my prayers were not going anywhere, so I decided to pray the Word. I began reading the book of Proverbs for about half an hour. Then a word that I never heard anyone shared jumped off the pages at me like lightening. *My son, fear thou the Lord and the king: and meddle not with them that are given to change.* (Proverbs 24:21)

The Lord started to deal with me about how He, the Lord, was not given to change. He said to me...*For I am the Lord, I change not...*Malachi 3:6. He further impressed on me that I should remember who He was...*Jesus Christ the same yesterday, and today, and forever. Hebrews 13:8.* He also reminded me that...*Heaven and earth shall pass away, but my words shall not pass away. (Mathew 24:35, Mark 13:31 and Luke 21:33).* The scripture emphatically states in 2nd Corinthians 13:1 that...*In the mouth of two or three witnesses shall every word be established.* 2nd Peter 3:9 *The Lord is not slack concerning his promise, as some men count slackness; but is longsuffering to us-ward, not willing that any should perish but that all should come to repentance.*

60

The Lord started to reassure me that he will not fail me in spite of my failures and shortcomings, because his Love is PERFECT to me, and I should not worry about him changing his love for me. God's love for us is not contingent upon if we live right today or tomorrow. No, his love is constant. We must not however spurn his love because he will not always chide, but is longsuffering to us, and will not allow our lives to be snared or taken.

When you *Work the Word* of God in prayer, your prayers will improve. The Word of God is creative. It is ever living, ever settling, and brings peace. John 1:1 said, *"In the beginning was the Word, and the Word was with God, and the Word was God."* What makes the word of God so effective is that it is living. Jesus *said I am the Living Bread that came down from heaven...*John 6:51, also affirms him as the *Living Water...*John 4:10. This means we can eat and drink of him and will not grow hungry or thirsty. No wonder the woman at the well when asked whether she would partake of the living water unequivocally said yes. Getting a good dose of the Living Water, which is Christ, will turn one into an instant believer and witness.

When you know the Word, the devil will have a hard time convincing and twisting your faith in God. I remember how in the midst of me writing this book, I was going through another of my most fiery trials yet. I remember driving home one night from service and the enemy attacked my mind in most accusatory ways ever. He said, "Don't you see God is turning your *wait* into a *weight*." He went on to let me know how foolish I was to be listening to my pastor and others who have "made it," and how their lives are "prosperous." The devil was having a field day between my ears. My mind was bombarded with every negative thought that only came from hell. I was so pressed down and frustrated I just felt like throwing in the towel and calling it a-day. But, thank God for a working knowledge of the Word of God. I will confess though that when I am at my wits end, and I feel like this God business and living for others need to go, I quickly get a reality check. The question I ask myself is who will have my heart if I let God alone and do my thing?

I have always lived with only two views as to whom we serve, God or the devil. I do not believe in living in the middle – there is no purgatory in my book. Therefore, to think that not serving the Lord is to serve the devil sets me straight every time even if it is on a subconscious level. I remember telling the devil *YES* my *wait* might feel like a *weight*, but contrary to your accusation, devil, *I WILL* wait on the Lord...*But they that wait upon the Lord shall renew their strength; they shall mount up with wings as eagles; they shall run, and not be weary; and they shall walk, and not faint* –Isaiah 40:31. Then I remembered how the scripture equates weight with sin, and I was not about to leverage my waiting on the Lord to sin, so the Word came with brute force against the devil's fiery dart and I heard in my spirit as it were the Angel of the Lord plundering the enemy by saying...*Wherefore seeing we also are compassed about with so great a cloud of witnesses, let us lay aside **every weight**, and the sin which doth so easily beset us, and let us run with patience the race that is set before us, Looking unto Jesus the author and finisher of our faith; who for the joy that was set before him endured the cross, despising the shame, and is set down at the right hand of the throne of God.*

I felt revived. I felt strength returning to my troubled and frustrated mind. I felt the need to fight again, all because of the living and creative Word that dwells on the inside. I would encourage every saint of God to use the Word of God as your most fierce weapon in prayer. ***Work it and watch it work for you!***

The clarion call comes shouting down the halls of time, *"For the word of God is quick, and powerful, and sharper than any twoedged sword, piercing even to the dividing asunder of soul and spirit, and of the joints and marrow, and is a discerner of the thoughts and intents of the heart."* (Hebrews 4:12) Jesus and all his disciples used the word and were victorious; therefore, let us follow their lead, and let the word work for us.

Sometimes people who should *"know"* better in the kingdom of God can challenge your faith instead of encouraging it. Let us revisit the Elijah and Elisha story. The sons of the prophets were aware of the soon departure of Elijah just as Elisha did. But, they made Elisha work for his enduring faith. They taunted him day and night about Elijah's soon departure. But Elisha was wholeheartedly resolute on receiving what the Lord had for him, so he had to put on spiritual blinders, and like a broken record kept saying, "I know, hold your peace." Elisha's persistence paid off because not only did he get the double portion sought, but he received the coveted mantle of Elijah -- The Mantle of sacrifice, authority and prayer. This situation can be compared to Jesus leaving his disciples, but giving them hope that he will never leave them comfortless, he would send them the comforter which is the Holy Ghost. History recorded the great outpouring of the Holy Ghost on the day of Pentecost in Acts 2, and it is still being outpoured some 2000 years later upon us. This is the reason why we can pray and endure such hard contradictions and trials with such grace. I believe Elisha understood the importance of the man and his mantle or the man and his prayer life; and to get Elijah's mantel, oh what an honor that was. I would encourage you to read on the life of Elijah and

Elisha in 2Kings 1-14. It will shed more light on what can become from a life given to prayer and consecration.

Prayer must also be offered in the faith knowing that God is, and that he is the hearer and answerer of prayers, and that he will fulfill his word. Here are examples of biblical characters who prayed, and I would highly recommend you read their prayers and gain strength from their approach:

Abraham's servant prayed to God, and God directed him to the person who should be wife to his master's son and heir (Gen. 24:10-20).

Jacob prayed to God, and God inclined the heart of his irritated brother, so that they met in peace and friendship (Gen. 32: 24-30; 33:1-4).

Samson prayed to God, and God showed him a well where he quenched his burning thirst, and so lived to judge Israel (Judg. 15:18-20).

David prayed, and God defeated the counsel of Ahithophel (2 Sam. 15:31; 16: 20-23; 17:14-23).

Daniel prayed, and God enabled him both to tell Nebuchadnezzar his dream and to give the interpretation of it (Dan. 2: 16-23).

Nehemiah prayed, and God inclined the heart of the king of Persia to grant him leave of absence to visit and rebuild Jerusalem (Neh. 1:11; 2:1-6).

Esther and Mordecai prayed, and God defeated the purpose of Haman, and saved the Jews from destruction (Esther 4:15-17; 6:7, 8).

The believers in Jerusalem prayed, and God opened the prison doors and set Peter at liberty, when Herod had resolved upon his death (Acts 12:1-12).

Paul prayed that the thorn in the flesh might be removed, and his prayer brought a large increase of spiritual strength, while the thorn perhaps remained (2 Cor. 12:7-10).

(Robinson's Job - Easton Bible Dictionary)

"Prayer is like the dove that Noah sent forth, which blessed him not only when it returned with an olive-leaf in its mouth, but when it never returned at all." (Robinson Job) Be encouraged. God took the time to preserve the entire 66 books of the bible for our learning, and within its pages are unlimited prayer resources. Let us use the Bible not just as a story book, or a history book, but rather a prayer book. The old Sunday school songs are still relevant today, if we simple apply their wisdom:

My bible and I, my bible and I, what a wonderful treasure, God gave us a measure. We will travel together, my bible and I.

The B I B L E - That's the book for me, I stand alone on the Word of God – The B I B L E

Read your bible, pray every day, pray every day, pray every day. Read your bible, pray every day, and you'll grow, grow, grow.

May the Lord Jesus Christ quicken His Words in your heart and give you a fresh revelation of His power through praying His life giving and life changing Words.

Insights and Prayer Points for Praying the Word in your life

1. Build in quality time to study the word of the Lord as you would any other priority in your life.
2. Attend your local church's bible study and be an active participant.
3. Teach a Bible study. It is a disciplined way to force you to study to show yourself approved unto God.
4. Start a bible study at home. A great manual is from own Sunday School book – even your child's Sunday School hand book can be used – it is starting point, right?
5. Memorize a verse or two each week. Use those verses in your prayer time and apply them to your daily devotion, and before you know it you will be relying on the Word for sustenance. Oh what a marvelous experience when you find yourself hooked to the Word of God, after all, you cannot separate the Lord from his Word.
6. Be prepared when you go to pray. Journal your prayers. Take your bible, a note pad, a pen and use them! No matter how insignificant a word you receive in prayer, note it. It just takes a seed to grow into an old Oak.
7. Here is another noble idea. Keep a notepad by your bedside at nights. When you maintain a healthy relationship with the Lord, He will visit you in your dreams. As soon as you rise, write down your dream(s). I have been given messages and songs in my dreams. When I fail to note it, I lose it. Not a nice feeling I tell you.
8. Create your sacred place to pray and read your bible. You never know, the Lord might draw alongside as he did with the disciples on the Emmaus road. I have made a personal decision not to have a TV in my bedroom, which is my prayer closet. I tried once to bring one in there after the terrorist attack on September 11, 2001, and I would not tell you how the Lord rebuked me for it. God will honor you when you honor Him.

Psalms 62

1. *Truly my soul waiteth upon God: from him cometh my salvation.*
2. *He only is my rock and my salvation; he is my defence; I shall not be greatly moved.*
3. *How long will ye imagine mischief against a man? ye shall be slain all of you: as a bowing wall shall ye be, and as a tottering fence.*
4. *They only consult to cast him down from his excellency: they delight in lies: they bless with their mouth, but they curse inwardly. Selah.*
5. *My soul, wait thou only upon God; for my expectation is from him.*
6. *He only is my rock and my salvation: he is my defence; I shall not be moved.*
7. *In God is my salvation and my glory: the rock of my strength, and my refuge, is in God.*
8. *Trust in him at all times; ye people, pour out your heart before him: God is a refuge for us. Selah.*
9. *Surely men of low degree are vanity, and men of high degree are a lie: to be laid in the balance, they are altogether lighter than vanity.*
10. *Trust not in oppression, and become not vain in robbery: if riches increase, set not your heart upon them.*
11. *God hath spoken once; twice have I heard this; that power belongeth unto God.*
12. *Also unto thee, O Lord, belongeth mercy: for thou renderest to every man according to his work.*

Chapter Four

Fourth Principle

Expect the Unexpected

Faith is taking the first step even when you don't see the whole staircase.
Dr. Martin Luther King, Jr.

It was in January of this year, in our month of consecration, that I was in deep intercessory prayer and I felt this urge to pray for our District Youth President, Rev. Omar Jolly. As I prayed the burden became more intense so like most students of prayer, when you go to pray, you try turn off all distractions. With tears streaming down, I reached over and turned on the cell phone and started to pray more earnestly for him. I remember expressing to the Lord how much I wanted to pray for Bro. Jolly in person, I even went as far as to say, please let him call me right know. Now, one must understand that although Bro. Jolly and I work together for the NY Metro-District, it is unusual for us to call each other on a regular basis. So, as I labored in prayer for him, within a few minutes the phone rang. To my utter amazement I saw "Omar Jolly" flash across my phone. I must confess I was floored. I almost had the same reaction like Rhoda in the book of Acts, where when they prayed for Peter's deliverance from prison, after the Lord released him, when he came to the gate to be let in, excitement

68

took a hold of Rhoda that she forgot to let him in. So, my first reaction was shock. I had forgotten that the only way to hear the person on the phone is to answer it. When I gathered my bearings, I answered the phone by saying, "Bro Jolly is that you, really you?" Of course he was taken aback and so calmly reassured me that "Yes", indeed it was him. He then explained how he felt a real urge to call me. Then I went on a roll explaining what had just happened. After all the nervous chatter, I proceeded to ask, "So Bro. Jolly may I pray for you?" Bro. Jolly answered, "Well Sis. Banks you said the Lord wanted you to pray for me, so here I am." And the rest is history.

The morale behind this real event shows the way we sometimes react to supernatural occurrences. One can begin to analyze my reaction, but the key here is, we have become so accustomed to operating in the natural realm, so that when we step into the supernatural realm, we act and react in the acute stress responses, typically the fight or flight syndrome, originated by Walter Cannon in the 1920's. Therefore, walking in readiness waiting for the unexpected will be something to become familiar with, just as in any other learned behavior. But let it be known that as you or I draw closer to the Lord, our expectancy level will become more heightened; hence, this seemingly elusive revival that we have been praying for will become a reality in the not so distant future. Will you join me in seeking the Lord, so that His reality will become ours?

"My soul, wait thou only upon God; for my expectation is from him. And I said, my strength is perished, and mine expectation is from Jehovah. For the earnest expectation of the creature waiteth for the manifestation of the sons of God. And now, Lord, what wait I for? My hope is in thee. If a man dies, shall he live again? All the days of my appointed time will I wait, till my change come." (*Psm 62:5; ASV. Lam. 3:18; Rom. 8:19, Psm. 39:7; Job 14:14*)

What is it that makes a man or woman develop a sense of expectation or hope in the face of great despair, unrest or confusion? That is what we seek as we take a deeper look at expectancy. According to Strong's Concordance, the Hebrew word translated expect means: qavah (*kaw-vaw'*) *to bind* together (perhaps by *twisting*), that is, *collect*; (figuratively) to *expect:* - gather (together), look, patiently, tarry, wait (for, on, upon). The other derivative is tiqvah (*tik-vaw'*) literally a *cord* (as an *attachment*); figuratively *expectancy:* - expectation ([-ted]), hope, live, thing that I long for.

I like the idea of hope and expectancy. It puts you on the edge of your seat, knowing any day now, something is about to happen. In Romans 4:16-24, Paul captured the true essence of what hope looked like in the life of Abraham. Verses 23 – 24 are especially applicable to us since it illustrates that we can experience similar hope even to the testing of our faith. Then, Proverbs 13: 12 states, *Hope deferred maketh the heart sick: but when the desire cometh, it is a tree of life.* This verse of scripture strengthens our assurance that our desires for Christ will always be satisfied. Let's reflect on the passage on hope in Romans 4: 16-24:

> *Therefore it is of faith, that it might be by grace; to the end the promise might be sure to all the seed; not to that only which is of the law, but to that also which is of the faith of Abraham; who is the father of us all; (As it is written, I have made thee a father of many nations,) before him whom he believed, even God, who quickeneth the dead, and calleth those things which be not as though they were. <u>Who against hope believed in hope, that he might become the father of many nations;</u>*

according to that which was spoken, So shall thy seed be. And being not weak in faith, he considered not his own body now dead, when he was about an hundred years old, neither yet the deadness of Sara's womb: He staggered not at the promise of God through unbelief; but was strong in faith, giving glory to God; And being fully persuaded that, what he had promised, he was able also to perform. And therefore it was imputed to him for righteousness. Now it was not written for his sake alone, that it was imputed to him; But for us also, to whom it shall be imputed, if we believe on him that raised up Jesus our Lord from the dead.

I was working in Bridgeport, CT in 2000. It was the year of change in every aspect of my life, not to mention the reorganization and restructure buzz words in corporate America. The financial company I worked for was going mean and lean, so every job that was deemed irrelevant was cut. The idea of last in - first out was the norm of the day. I was hired in August '98 as a part of the change management team. We reengineered and eliminated jobs without much question. Today your department was there and tomorrow you were gone. That was as drastic as it got. You talk about red-lining, that company did it. Then it came to my job – air marked – elimination. Now that's what you call lean. So, one day as I was driving home and was wondering where do I go from here? There it was as I turned on to the bend on Interstate (95) in Stamford CT, I saw a huge billboard with the words–EXPECT THE UNEXPECTED! I do not know if it was there all along but all I could remember is oops there it is. And there it was, my Word from the Lord: ***Walk in Expectancy, I will turn your Captivity.***

You talk about renewed hope and drive; it was as though I got a shot of energy booster drugs intravenously. I felt a peace

71

that passeth all human understanding, and a calm assurance that the Lord was working it out for me. I did not know how or I did not know when this was going to happen, but I just hoped against hope. Within weeks of me seeing the sign, the word from the Lord came to life – I got a job offer that paid over 20% more than I previously made and it was less than 7 minutes away from my home. Sometimes God speaks and works in mysterious ways His wonders to perform.

I just sense an urge to pray for you right now. *Lord Jesus, Creator of the ends of the earth, shine forth on your children right now. Let us know assuredly that you are working on our behalf. I am reminded that you are the God of Abraham, Isaac and Jacob. They staggered not at your promises, but believed that through their perplexities and affliction, you would bring them through. Remember us and hear us when we call, in Jesus' name. Amen!*

I would like to entitle this other testimony as "*My Miracle on Delta Flight 5884.*" Sometimes the devil makes you to believe that your situation was devil sent when in truth it was God sent to bring out the best in you as well as to make propitiation for others.

It was in July 2008, I was on a flight destined for disaster - Delta flight 5884. Before I share this miracle, let me give a little background information. I had a 6 a.m. flight from White Plains, NY to Indiana. I woke up at 5.15 a.m. and made it to the airport by 5:40 a.m. miraculously! The front desk refused to check me in. I was told to go to the gate with my unchecked luggage. I heard over the PA system final call to Indiana. In summary, I skipped many passengers, passed security without being checked – went up to the flight attendant, and told her I was to be on the plane that announced the final call. I was given clearance with a large heavy suitcase, not a regular carry-on, without a hassle. I believe the Lord actually shut their eyes against the luggage.

I was one of the last persons to board the flight. After being seated, with my nerves all over the place, the pilot announced that there would be a 25 minute delay due to inclement weather. Whew...I needed those few minutes to gather my bearings, but that was short lived. It was raining cats and dogs not to mention lightning and thunder. Then a few minutes later the pilot announced they got the OK to take off. Strange don't you think!

Well, this is where I personally believe the Lord had it all planned for me to be on that plane. Not even 5 minutes in flight, all hell broke loose–literally. In the midst of the flight, the atmosphere began to misbehave. We went right into thick black clouds - I guess that's what you call a storm cloud. The plane began to shake violently, then dipped precipitously, and began to shake like a drunken man. People were holding on to the back of the seats and bracing themselves for dear life. If I told you I was not scared I would be lying through my teeth.

In the dead grip of silence, I started to pray inwardly with tears streaming down my face then it all happened. Silent prayers became gut wrenching, intercessory prayer. I cared not who heard or thought of me as being crazy. Hey, a dying woman will do any and everything to save her life. I started by calling on the name of Jesus, which shifted gears into pleading the Blood of Jesus on the top of my voice. I commanded Angels to take over the flight. I rebuked every demon known and unknown in Jesus' name. I sent Angels in the cockpit, on the wings and in/outside of the plane. I commanded the winds to cease in Jesus' name. All this time, nobody, can I say nobody, uttered a word! This went on for 3- 5 minutes well...I tell you those few minutes were like an eternity when you are in a plane destined for disaster.

73

Then suddenly there was calm, and the pilot came over the speaker and said we just got clearance to take another route to our destination. I tell you after that there were clear skies and a smooth ride to Atlanta for the connecting flight to Indiana. Don't tell me that God does not work miracles. We went from a violent storm to clear skies in minutes. Then out of the blue, a little boy traveling with his dad, blurred out, "Dad, did you see the demon on the flight." His father was so shocked, he hushed the little boy and said, "Don't say anything." Need I say more?

At the end of the first leg of the flight one of the two male flight attendants came over to me and asked me if I was Apostolic Pentecostal. I told him unequivocally – YES! He told me he knew because he could only remember how his mom, who was raised in Jamaica, and who attended an apostolic church pled the blood of Jesus the way I did. Then the other attendant came over and asked me when I would be returning from my trip and I told him on Monday morning. He said "Good!" that's his next flight back to White Plains, and he would be delighted to have me on-board. Incidentally, they were the very attendants on the connected flight into Indiana from Atlanta. Coincidental - Hardly! Before I exited the plane they gave me a bag of goodies and a big hug. That was a miracle, and I give Jesus all the glory and praise.

I tell this true story to say you must expect God to answer your prayers when **_you_** pray. Jesus said in Mark 11:24 *Therefore I say unto you, What things so ever ye desire, **_when ye pray_**, believe that ye receive them, and ye shall have them.* When YE pray, is the same as saying when YOU pray. It was in prayer that the Lord gave me this illumination on this particular verse of scripture Mark 11:24.

He told me that _**I should believe in MY PRAYERS, because if I do not then NO ONE else will.**_ I am not sure if

74

someone gave me a million dollars if it would send off the same amount of endorphins in me like this scripture did in my spirit. I said to the Lord, "*do you really mean that I was not really believing in my prayers all these years...?*" and I could hear as it were a big "*YEAH*" with an attitude in my head. I asked the Lord pardon and promised to believe in my own prayers from that day forward. How can I ask others to pray and believe when I am not doing the same? That is pure hypocrisy.

So here again, God allowed me to practice what was taught and to assess if any learning was applied. I remember in January 2009, we had our month of consecration. We fasted and prayed for the month which culminated in all-night prayer. The presence and power of the Lord was so real, it was as if one could touch as it were the face of God. That was how all consuming the presence of the Lord was in the place. Several weeks later, we had a Holy Ghost Rally with Rev. Eli Hernandez as the evangelist; and oh how he preached the word of Faith and prophesied of the miracles the Lord would do for us. I was on cloud nine with faith and hope in the Lord. My confessions were on point until...

Well, it was in March of '09, I noticed that when my arm brushed against my right breast it was unusually tender and oversized. When I did myself examination, I felt a lump the size of my knee cup. That's the only way I could describe it. It was huge. The same time I remembered the Word of the Lord and I grabbed the anointed oil and anointed my breast and commanded that lump to go in Jesus' name. Several days passed and it dawned on me that the lump was gone. I checked and rechecked and it was gone.

I was so elated I started to testify of the miraculous power of the Lord. Many were encouraged and even others told me of their miracles due to my testimony. I remember telling my testimony at our NY Metro District Ladies Day session in April '09. After the service, a sister came to me and told me that instantaneously after I shared my testimony the Lord miraculously healed her of breast cancer. She went on to inform me that I was the third person she had shared her recent diagnosis with and she was convinced of the Lord's healing. We blessed the Lord Jesus Christ and left it there.

My friends, when you openly confess your miracle, expect the unexpected on both sides of the spectrum. The devil will try to defy the Lord and your faith by allowing symptoms to re-appear. But the devil is a liar and the father of it. The next month the breast was swollen all over again. My thoughts were, "devil I will not have it. You will not mess with my miracle. I rebuke you in Jesus' name." I became so angry at the devil, if he was in flesh he would have been dead. I mean minced meat DEAD.

He waged a war on my mind and even intercepted my dreams. That creep told me you have cancer. He said you believe the Lord would heal you and so many are still sick. Do you think you are that special? What audacity of that kingdom-less, homeless and toothless punk. He is a projector of filthiness that both God and men have rejected. He is that thing that will be discarded like trash and burn forever. I want satan that old devil to know unequivocally that I hate him, and will stand in agreement with the Lord Jesus Christ to destroy his works every chance I get. Let it be known that *I do not like the devil,* to put it mildly.

So, I decided to go to the doctor to see what this symptom might be as I had this calm assurance that the Lord had already healed me. When the doctor tested me, you should have seen her eyes. Just looking on her would put cancer in you. She said Ms. Banks I do not like this. She said this thing in your

76

breast is massive. You must go and take a mammogram and sonogram as soon as possible. In fact, she called and made the appointment for me right there in the office. But for some reason I was not scared. Concerned, "Yes," but scared and nervous, "No."

So, I went by myself to do this test. A friend of mine after I told her that I went for the test all by myself said, "*Sis. You are one brave soul.*" I went in, did my prep and waited to be called. The nurse called and I went in and she did her thing. I was then told to sit on the outside. I waited for about 15 minutes then I was called in again. She walked into the room with the X-Ray of my left breast, (I thought the issue was with the right breast, now I know the devil is a liar) with an area circled. She said we have to take some more pictures of the circled area. Now the devil started, "*told you...you have cancer.*" For some reason the nurse stepped out of the room, which gave me a few minutes to set that devil straight. I told him to go to hell from whence he came in Jesus' name. Again walked in the nurse and I noticed that she had a Jamaican accent. She spoke my language. I said to her, "*Nurse, I just want to assure you that you are not going to find anything in my breast. I plead the Blood of Jesus over me right now in Jesus' name.*" She simply looked at me as if to say you go girl or there goes another nut. Hey, you have to safeguard your expectations and hope in God.

When she was finished I was told to have a seat in the waiting area until they did their consultation. About half an hour later she called me in. She said we must send you to do a sonogram. Fear started to raise his ugly head. I started to feel a bit uneasy and nervous. There and then I checked my email and someone had posted a scripture on Face Book... Jeremiah 29:11 *For I know the thoughts that I think toward you, saith the Lord, thoughts of peace, and not of evil, to give you an expected end.*

77

This Word of the Lord came right in time. I held on the words. *The Lord's thoughts are for good towards me.* I kept saying it over and over in my mind. The Word of God is truly living and it will breathe life into any dying situation.

After another long wait I was ushered into a different area and was now under a different medical practitioner. She did her examination. A few minutes later after she walked out without saying a word, the radiologist walked in. She had a very puzzled look on her face. She blurted out, "Miss Banks, are you *sure* (emphasis on the *SURE*) there was something in your breast?" I asked why, she said, "after reading the doctor's report which stated that we should be looking for a 3cm mass in the right breast, we have assessed and cannot find any abnormality." She went on to describe the size by making an "O" with her thumb and index finger to show the size mass she was looking for. She then said, "why we kept you here so long and did the battery of tests is because we are searching for the mass that your doctor indicated we should look for." She then looked at me again and said "are you sure that there was something in your breast?" as if to question my sanity. She said, "when you see your doctor tell him as far as the tests show, there was no cause for concern; so please get dressed and you are free to go home."

I know you are wondering what was my response…to be honest I was at a loss for words. I just stood there and took it all in. When I walked outside I was on cloud nine to say the least. I thanked the Lord and gave him all the glory for His manifold blessings towards me. To God be the glory great things he hath done! Rev. Jeff Arnold said *"Expectancy Level - High!"* Your miracle is on the way. *Believe it! Expect it! Expect the Unexpected in your life today, in Jesus' name!*

"Father, I ask you to reassure your dear children at this time. Let them know you are concerned about their concerns.

Give them peace of mind and a calm assurance that You who started this good work in them will complete it, in Jesus' name. Amen."

Insights and Prayer Points for
Praying with Expectancy

1. You must believe that He is, and He is a rewarder of those who diligently seek Him.
2. Expect the Lord to come by unannounced.
3. Expect God to use you in any way He deems fit. Be it in public ministry, administrative or support roles, expect to use your talents for His glory.
4. Practice to live by faith and not by sight. You will notice that your speech will become positive and your prayers will become forceful. This is due to the fact that your reliance is on the Lord and not on yourself.
5. Praise and worship God like you just received a million dollars. It will put pep in your step, and a bundle of joy in your heart!
6. Last but certainly not least, speak and live by faith. Exercise your confidence in God. In other words, put God to the test and watch Him work on your behalf. It will surprise you how your perspective changes as you learn to trust the Lord for everything.

Psalms 150

1. Praise ye the Lord. Praise God in his sanctuary: praise him in the firmament of his power.
2. Praise him for his mighty acts: praise him according to his excellent greatness.
3. Praise him with the sound of the trumpet: praise him with the psaltery and harp.
4. Praise him with the timbrel and dance: praise him with stringed instruments and organs.
5. Praise him upon the loud cymbals: praise him upon the high sounding cymbals.
6. Let every thing that hath breath praise the Lord. Praise ye the Lord.

Chapter Five

Fifth Principle

Remember, God Gets the Glory!

He (Abraham) staggered not at the promise of God through
unbelief; but was strong in faith, giving glory to God.
Romans 4:20

I was taught the quickest way to get into the presence of the Lord is through praise and worship. I have made it a mantra of mine to pray and ask the Lord to make me a true worshipper. I have practiced in my walk with the Lord over some thirty years to be thankful for the smallest of blessings so when the "big" ones come, my praise and worship will echo the same.

"That God in all things may be glorified." (1 Pet. 4:11). The glory of God is a steadying thread which must run through all our actions. "Whether therefore ye eat or drink, or whatsoever ye do, do all to the glory of God." (1 Cor. 10:31). The glory that God has in himself, is his intrinsic glory. Glory is essential to the Godhead, as light is to the sun: he is called the "God of glory." Acts 7:2. Glory is the sparkling of the Deity; it is so co-natural to the Godhead, that God cannot be God without it. A king is a man without his regal ornaments, when his crown and royal robes are taken away; but God's glory is such an essential part of his being, that he cannot be God without it. , "My glory I will not give to another."(Isa. 48:11) David reminded us in 1 Chron. 16:29,

"Give unto the Lord the glory due unto his name." And, 1 Cor. 6:20, "Glorify God in your body, and in your spirit." The glory we give God is nothing else but our lifting up his name in the world, and magnifying him in the eyes of others. Phil. 1:20, "Christ shall be magnified in my body."

My former pastor told us "stay in the spout where the glory comes out." I took that to literally mean, sit on the front seat in church and when the anointing from the Word comes, it will hit me first with gale like wind-force, and the others seated behind me get the tail end. You see when the word of conviction comes and I find myself wanting, because of where I am seated, I can make my way to the altar without eyes of condemnation stopping me. Try sitting on the front seat, I assure you most of your distractions in worship will dissipate sooner than you think. You do not have to agree with me, but I know I am right! That calls for a lol (laugh-out-loud) response.

Whenever the Lord allows you to do something of value, and you and others derive benefit from it, remember the source of your blessing – *God Gets the Glory*. Even God in his *"Godness,"* if there is such a word, gave thanks by patting himself on his own back as it were and declared it is *good*. Genesis 1:10 is one of the many verses that shows God calling what he created "*good*."

As I thought about how to anchor or finish this book, I opened my Bible for a Word from the Lord, and the Lord led me to Philippians 4:6-10, 13. I hope I can do justice to explain how these verses gave me assurance to give God the Glory. Let us read the verses:

> *Be careful for nothing; but in everything by prayer and*
> *supplication with thanksgiving let your requests be made*
> *known unto God. And the peace of God, which passeth*

all understanding, shall keep your hearts and minds through Christ Jesus.

Finally, brethren, whatsoever things are true, whatsoever things are honest, whatsoever things are just, whatsoever things are pure, whatsoever things are lovely, whatsoever things are of good report; if there be any virtue, and if there be any praise, think on these things. Those things, which ye have both learned, and received, and heard, and seen in me, do: and the God of peace shall be with you. But I rejoiced in the Lord greatly, that now at the last your care of me hath flourished again; wherein ye were also careful, but ye lacked opportunity. I can do all things through Christ which strengtheneth me.

Paul spoke about how we should be anxious or careful for nothing, but to utilize the vehicle of prayer and petition to bring our concerns to the Lord. He said you will get peace that passes all human understanding which comes in Jesus Christ. But Paul made a sad commentary on verse 10 of Philippians 6 and the last clause... ***but ye lacked opportunity.*** Lacked opportunity to do what? To take care of his needs. Allow me to use the term "lack opportunity" in the sense of our worship and praise to the Lord. Could it be that we lack opportunity to give glory to God because we are caught up with our own desires to satisfy our carnal needs? That thought brought to mind Michal, King David's first, wife, when she disdained him for what she thought to be crude and extravagant worship.

A New Level of Worship

Before I attempt to discuss a new concept on worship, I want you to refrain from coming to a conclusion before you read the entire subject matter. The information shared has no bearing historically on any group or social order. With that said, one of the newest saying on the streets or among the learned when they see certain behavior that is not copasetic with their norm, they would say that is "*so ghetto*" or "street," coupled with the shaking of the head with disgust. But please allow me to share another view on "so-ghetto" or rather "so getto."

According to Wikipedia.com the word "ghetto" actually comes from the word "getto" or "gheto". It is used to describe behaviors that happen in the street, or in certain neighborhoods, or among minority groups. Those who have been to finishing school, and those who understand the power or notion of social graces would definitely faint, as it were, when "ghetto" style behaviors are displayed especially in public. So let us dig further into my new concept of ghetto worship.

The Lord has some strange ways of dealing with me and using what I call modern day parables, to bring out a point. I am a very creative thinker, and at times, only a physical or mental picture does the job for me. (May I interject here and encourage you to know who you are, and once you find you, love "*you*" and operate there, as opposed to trying to be like someone else.) So, this is what I feel the Lord brought to my mind. He said I need some "*Getto*" worshippers. A person who is truly Ghetto will spell Ghetto, Getto. I said, "*Lord, what in the world are you talking about?*" He said, "look on the word more carefully and dissect it." Well I did and the result was "*Get to*". *I thought, "What! You mean getto is really get to?"* So the concept of Getto worshipper comes into play. We GET TO worship the LORD of the Universe. I must confess I am still in awe of the idea that I truly **_Get To_** worship the KING OF KINGS and the LORD OF LORDS. This is mind blowing to say the least!

I feel the Lord is saying in my spirit, I need some people who will lose their inhibition and be fill with inebriation which means *to make drunk; intoxicate, to exhilarate or stupefy as with alcohol; in other words, to become a drunkard.* (I tell you I am going crazy right about now as I type this piece with the prospects that God wants me to worship until people think I am drunk or have lost my God given mind.)

The sophisticated both spiritually and morally, and the well learned who cannot seem to burst a sweat in worship may be thinking, it does not take all that. May I ask then, how is it that this same group of people can plan a Super Bowl Party, invite those of the same great social upbringing, and then go crazy over a quarterback who runs with a piece of cow-hide football around a field. In the same way, how can soccer fans get so glued to television set and watch the World Cup and lose their God given mind over a man scoring a goal. Am I saying that you should not have a good time, of course not, but at the same time do not look down on someone because he or she wants to express his or her love for the Master. We really need to get our priorities straight. The only PERSON in the universe that should get all that glory and praise is the One who made us all, the Lord God Almighty

So then, God is looking for some people who will become so *"getto"* in worship, understanding that they **_GET TO_** worship the KING of Kings and the LORD of Lords, the Almighty God, Creator of the ends of the earth. Please excuse me; I am taking a praise break right about now! Hallelujah! Thank You Jesus, Glory to God. Father I love with my whole heart and mind, with all my soul, with all my strength. I give you all the praise. I blow kisses to you, I feel a Yadah (*out stretched hands with palms upward)* praise coming on. I bless your Holy Name Jesus. Don't just sit there, join me in worship and praise to our God. Hallelujah! O glory!

So, here David started to think of the Goodness of Jehovah God and how he delivered him out the hand of Goliath, and out of the jaws of the lion, and out of the claws of the bear. And He began to say, "I will bless the Lord at all times and praise shall continually be in my mouth." Then he looked at how the Lord brought him from watching sheep, smelling like sheep, sleeping under the stars with the sheep to having ivory palaces as his home. He could have any bride he desired and those whom he did not desire, like Michal, (had to throw that in for good measure) and she did not like the fact that he worshipped the Lord with all his might. I believe David understood the concept of being a "getto" worshipper. Of course, Michal did not understand what made David tick. She only saw the opulence, but not the God behind it all. Let us read the account of David's rendezvous with God when he brought back the ark to Jerusalem:

> *And David danced before the LORD with all [his] might; and David [was] girded with a linen ephod. So David and all the house of Israel brought up the ark of the LORD with shouting, and with the sound of the trumpet. And as the ark of the LORD came into the city of David, Michal, Saul's daughter, looked through a window, and saw king David leaping and dancing before the LORD; and she despised him in her heart. Then David returned to bless his household. And Michal the daughter of Saul came out to meet David, and said, How glorious was the king of Israel to-day, who uncovered himself to-day in the eyes of the handmaids of his servants, as one of the vain fellows shamelessly uncovereth himself! And David said to Michal, [It was] before the LORD, who chose me before thy father, and before all his house, to appoint me ruler over the people of the LORD, over Israel: therefore will I play before the LORD. And I shall yet be more vile than thus, and shall be base in my own sight: and by the maid-servants which thou hast spoken of, by them shall I be had in honor. Therefore Michal the daughter of Saul had no child until the day of her death. (2Samuel 6:14-16 & 20-23)*

The scripture said that David danced (*whirl)* before the Lord with all his might. Might in Hebrew mean (*oze) strength* (*force, security, majesty, praise*): - boldness, loud, might, and power. Michal even gave us a more vivid picture of David's actions when in disdain she described his worship. She likened him to a vile fellow, and used words like shamelessly uncovering himself. The Hebrew defined these words as follows:

Vain-fellow – (rake) *empty*; figuratively *worthless: -* emptied (-ty), vain (fellow, man).

Shamelessly uncovering himself - Galah *gaw-law)* to *denude* (especially in a disgraceful sense); by implication to *exile* (captives being usually *stripped*); figuratively to *reveal:* advertise, appear, bewray, bring, (carry, lead, go) captive (into captivity), depart, disclose, discover, exile, be gone, open, plainly, publish, remove, reveal, X shamelessly, shew, surely, tell, uncover. (Strong"s Concordance)

Basically she said to David, *you disgrace me by the way how you deface the crown by whirling about in the nude. And to make matters worse, you did it before the ladies.* David was quick in his response. He said *you have not seen anything yet. I am going to be wilder and crazier than ever. And the audience that you mentioned me dancing before will be honored to see their king worship the God of Heaven, unreservedly...*

This kind of Davidic mind set on worshipping and glorifying God, to me, epitomizes the true essence of what a "getto" worshipper looks and feels like. J. Moss, a gospel singer, puts it this way: *"There's a praise on the inside that can't keep to myself There's a holler stirrin' up from the depths of my soul So excuse me if I seem a little giddy or maybe even strange. But praise is the way I say Thanks!"*

Trivializing worship is not good at any level. Let us be aware that God is the ultimate judge on true worship, and obviously, He did not like Michal's view on David's exuberance in worship. His punishment for her behavior was barrenness for the rest of her life. *Lord, please help us not to bring a curse on ourselves because we fail to recognize and value true worship.*

On the day of Pentecost, one hundred and twenty persons made such an uproar in Jerusalem that others came from near and far to see what made the men and women behave so *"getto"* or *drunken* as stated in Acts 2. Don't they know that the learned do not behave like that? I promise you, if we could start worshipping God with some spiritual inebriation, you will see people requesting salvation as in Acts 2:37...*Men and brethren, what shall we do?* Then we will be able to preach the gospel message like Peter did in verse 38... *Repent, and be baptized every one of you in the name of Jesus Christ for the remission of sins, and ye shall receive the gift of the Holy Ghost.* After the people heard the word, they acted immediately: *Then they...were baptized: and the same day there were added unto them about three thousand souls.*

Could it be that we are the ones stopping this end time revival because we refuse to worship God in the way that will attract others to Lord Jesus Christ? I submit to you, if we ever sit down and truly think about the manifold blessings of the Lord to us, we would really begin to praise and give GOD THE GLORY for all He has done for us. We would be like Zacchaeus in Luke 19:2-9, who gave back to all whom he stole from. Jesus commented on a heart that was released from pride and wickedness, likening his house to that of the son of Abraham. Lord help us! May I ask you the million-dollar question? When was the last time you *"getto"* worshipped your God? Let us pray:

Father, we have sinned against you and our generation in not giving you the glory due unto your name. Please have mercy and forgive us our sins. We ask that you release us from pride and covetousness, which steals your praise and glory. We ask you to wash us. Lord, help us to be true worshippers and create in us a heart like David to worship you who is the source of ALL our strength and life. Bless us as we attempt to be "getto" worshippers, understanding that we simply **GET TO** *worship you who alone deserve all our praise. We give you ALL THE GLORY AND HONOR NOW AND FOREVE. These mercies we ask in Jesus' name, AMEN!*

A Lesson from Mary Magdalene

Another character that resonates with me is Mary Magdalene whom the Lord cast seven demons out of. She in my estimation holds a special place in the heart of the Lord because of her act of worship. We have read many accounts of Jesus healing many women of diverse diseases but he only mentioned in Mark 14:9 "...*wheresoever this Gospel shall be preached throughout the whole world, this also that she hath done shall be spoken of for a memorial of her.*"

In my research on the subject of true worship, I began to pay special attention to the things that are said about the worshiper. In the case of Mary Magdalene, she came prepared to shower her master with the best kind of worship she felt would do justice for all He had done for her. The pride and joy of any woman is the beauty of her hair. She spends countless hours grooming it to make it her personal crown jewel. So Mary decided what better sacrifice, what better offering of love, but to wash His feet with her hair. Then she looked around her room and her eyes could not pass over her most costly perfume,

90

Spikenard, the Prada or the Chanel of our day. Let me interject here and share some interesting information I found on the plant spikenard. "Spikenard[2] is an aromatic rhizome. The therapeutic properties of spikenard oil are anti-inflammatory, anti-pyretic, antiseptic...and tonic...It was obtained as a luxury in ancient Egypt, the Near East, and Rome, where it was the main ingredient of the perfume *nardinium.*"

In an article I read entitled "A bottle of Spikenard, very costly[3]" the author cited one Prof. Shaff which I thought would give insight to the cost of the ointment which Mary held so dear, and I quote:

> By the 'ointment' we are to understand rather a liquid perfume than what we commonly know as ointment. The alabaster box was rather in the shape of a flask or vase, and the breaking of the box (***Mark 14:3***) signifies the opening of its tyings and seals by which the precious odors were confined. Judas' words of dissatisfaction furnish us a clue respecting the costliness of this perfume, for he says that it "might have been sold for three hundred *denarii.*" A *denarius,* translated "penny" in *vs. 5,* is represented as being the average daily wages at that time--"a penny *[denarius]* a day." (***Matt. 20:2.***) If we compare these values with present money values, counting farm labor at fifty cents a day (which is certainly a moderate valuation), the three hundred *denarii* would be the equivalent in wages of one hundred and fifty dollars *($150)* of our currency. Thus we see that the perfume was indeed "very costly." This was nearly a pint of the perfume, a Roman pound being

---

[2] *Healinghandsapothecary.com/Spikenard.html*
[3] *www.agsconsulting.com/htdbv5/r2447.htm*

twelve ounces. Nor need we question the possibility of perfumes being so expensive, for even to-day we have a counterpart in value in the attar of roses made in the far East. It is claimed that four hundred thousand (400,000) full-grown roses are used to _produce one ounce of this perfume,_ which, in its purity, sells as high as one hundred dollars *($100)* an ounce, or twelve hundred dollars *($1,200)* for the quantity used by Mary in anointing our Lord. It is said that Nero was the first of the Emperors to indulge in the use of costly perfumes for his anointing; but one much more worthy of tribute, homage and anointing with a sweet perfume was the "Prince of the kings of the earth," whom Mary had the honor to anoint.

The scriptures said in John 12:3...*Then took Mary a pound of ointment of spikenard, very costly, and anointed the feet of Jesus, and wiped His feet with her hair: and the house was filled with the odour of the ointment."* Mark 14:3 positioned it this way: *"And being in Bethany in the house of Simon the leper, as he sat at meat, there came a woman having an alabaster box of ointment of spikenard very precious; and she brake the box, and poured it on his head."* Jesus mentioned how the anointing was for his burial, which in my estimation it is safe to say that He knew what Mary was truly doing. I believe Mary just wanted to express her love for her Master in the best way possible. So in keeping true to my new definition of Getto, I see that the spirit of "get-to" worship got into her. She remembered how the Lord cast out seven demons (Mark 16:9) out of her. One of which could have been Pride. So with a reservoir of tears she washed his feet, then she pulled down her hair– her glory – and used it to dry his feet. Oh what an act of worship!

Indulge me for a moment here, Mary did not just cry, she hollered. Have you ever gone through something that caused you to really cry? Or, have you ever wept in the presence of the Lord and the texture of tissue was not able to sustain all the excretion coming from your eyes, nose and mouth. You had to reach for super strength paper towel or a wash cloth. That is how I believe Mary's tears were able to wash his feet.

I have been there where it seems like every emotion inside of you begins to cry. I mean gut wrenching tears. I believe if she was silent with her act it would not have caught the disciples' attention and caused them to become indignant. Do you remember how Hannah was ridiculed and judged by Eli for her cries or lack thereof? I believe that the day in question, Hannah had cried so hard she had in essence lost her voice, and was called a drunk, because someone did not understand the power of weeping.

The act of crying is usually HEARD long before one SEES the tears. Think about a baby who is hungry or in need of a diaper change. The care giver gets into action very fast to avoid the screams of a hurting child. Some adjectives and/or synonyms for crying tears are bitter, gut wrenching, out of the recesses of the soul, bottom of the heart, wailing, screaming, screeching, chilling, blood curdling, lament, howling, bewail, sob, bawl, yell, scream, shriek, shout, bellow, roar, yell…by this time you have a resemblance as to why the disciples were indignant.

I am about to share a part of my live that I did not want to share but how can I truly express what weeping looks and feels like without being transparent. I pray this testimony will help you as you face your day of trouble.

Over twenty years ago, I went through a divorce. Yes, I was divorced, hated the situation but I would not exchange the experience gained in that it propelled me into a new life, and unique ministry. You can allow your situation to make you bitter or better. I choose the latter. My entire paradigm changed after this experience, which I will share if the Lord so grace me to write in my next book. The word of God figuratively put on flesh for me from that day on.

I remember one of the "**_many_**" days when my heart refused to stop crying, and I decided to go to church to pray, which usually equated to I am going to church to cry. I got to church pretty early because I did not want to disturb anyone with my grief. I found a place on the choir loft, buried my head into tons of tissues as it were and just cried my heart out to God. I was told *to cast my cares on him for he careth for me*; right? I did not know someone else was in the church building. It was a wonderful and faithful deacon who was doing his duties. Friends, I was in one of my weeping and wailing frame of mind, because I literally felt like my heart, my head and my entire body was falling apart. I was in a truly melting mode. Then all of a sudden, I was startled out on my wits by a hand tapping me on my shoulder. When I looked up it was Bro. Deacon. And he said something to this effect, *"why are you crying like someone is beating you."* People, thank God for the Holy Ghost, and for His holy angels which were sent to minister unto me that day, because I felt like telling him to go jump into the lake and leave me alone, for want of a better expression; but, no I did not, I am a Christian, hurting mind you, but a Christian nonetheless. With much grace I mustered the courage and said "I will be fine, thank you." Now you want a case to argue on "paradoxical," my thoughts verse my speech would be a classic.

The scriptures speaks of out of your belly shall flow rivers of living water. God help us to weep again! That day I experienced God in a different way, and to be honest, at the end of that day, I felt my heart began to heal. May I encourage you not to be afraid to cry i.e. *bawl*. Let us pause here for a second I feel the need to minister to a gentleman who is reading this section right now. You, yes you Mr. Gentleman, can I remind you that one great traits of being called "gentle" is your ability to feel a sense of compassion. It is impossible to be moved with compassion and not express it, and I mean with tears! Let me remind you that the Gentleman of all Gentlemen wept, and his name is **Jesus Christ**. (Madam don't feel left out, our nick name is cry baby. *For this time only we will take it as a compliment– smile*.) I pray that the Lord will send us more men who will weep between the porch and altar for the issues that face our hurting world. The Prophet Joel puts it this way, *Let the priests, the ministers of the Lord, weep between the porch and the altar, and let them say, Spare thy people, O Lord, and give not thine heritage to reproach, that the heathen should rule over them: wherefore should they say among the people, Where is their God?* (Joel 2:17)

Let us double back to the perfume that Mary brought with her to anoint her Master. What caught my attention about Spikenard was that it had therapeutic properties such as anti-inflammatory, anti-pyretic, and antiseptic values. I am not a medical professional, but I believe the Lord knew what He would face during the scourging process, and I felt he gave me this insight on it so I would like to share it. He made man, so he knew how infectious yea, deadly, the saliva could be from a sick person for example. So knowing the future and how He would subject himself to be spat upon, and to have a crown of thorns rammed into his head, Jesus allowed Mary the honor to do the pre-purification process, so his body would ward off any early inflammation or any corruption that would occur during or after scourging. The scriptures had to be fulfilled when it said in Psalms 16:10, *For thou wilt not leave my soul in hell; **neither*** *wilt thou suffer thine Holy One to see corruption.*

Judas and the others were indignant against Mary's act of worship and love for her master. I do not even believe that they understood her actions to say the least. Some religious folks have great insight but are grossly blinded towards the things of God. Paul echoed a similar sentiment in 1Corinthians 2:14. *But the natural man receiveth not the things of the Spirit of God: for they are foolishness unto him: neither can he know them, because they are spiritually discerned.* They can only comprehend the natural but the supernatural they scoff at. Mark 14 started out with the Jewish leaders seeking to kill Jesus. Even His disciples who should know better got caught up in worldly anti worship trends and scoffed at Mary's act of worship. Noting Jesus' rebuke of his disciples to *let her alone*, reminded me of how he had to chide the same group of disciples for forbidding little children that came unto him. What the Lord shared with me on the subject of the disciples stopping the children from coming to Him is rather troubling. The disciples were acting as Jesus' bodyguard, and putting Jesus in a celebrity status. Jesus caught on to that spirit of separation and isolation, not to mention respect of persons, and rebuked the spirit sharply. The disciples were treating Jesus as a superstar as it were, and he would not have it. Jesus wants an open door policy so all his children can come unto Him.

What I perceive the devil wants to do is to bring back the spirit of the dark ages where only a certain sect would have access to the Word of God, and the laity would have to be in submission and subservient to their bidding. I see the spirit of legalism standing at the door of worship and barring the children of God from truly worshipping the God of Heaven who is Jesus Christ. Leaders, I submit to you, if you allow people free access to Jesus Christ, your job of counseling people on how to live

96

morally will literally cease. I am even audacious enough to say that there will be a line of people at your door requesting your guidance as to how to channel their passion to do great works for Christ. Do not keep Jesus away from the people. Be as it were a concierge or doorkeeper and graciously escort people to Him. The Apostle Paul understood this concept very well and throughout the epistles communicated his passion for the believers to know Christ and his love for them and to be filled with the fullness of God. (Eph. 3:14-19) Under God, I rebuke that anti-Christ and anti-worship spirit right now in Jesus' name. I proclaim liberty for God's people to worship freely their Maker. *Lord Jesus, please allow your righteous indignation to arise into the hearts of your leaders and allow them to lead your people into true apostolic worship in Jesus' name.*

In conclusion, it is incumbent on us who profess to be worshippers, and those who are seeking to become true worshippers of our Lord Jesus Christ, to remember that whatever we do in word or deed, we must do all to the glory and honor of Him who has called us out of darkness into this marvelous light. No matter how insignificant it might seem to you, when the Lord does something for you or for anyone else for that matter, train yourself to be thankful with a grateful heart. Remember our new *"get-to"* worship philosophy. Let us put it into action starting now! I feel impressed to share with you one of Jesus' parables of the healing of the ten lepers. Please read observantly on how the leper who returned to give thanks reacted when he saw that he was healed:

> *And they lifted up their voices, and said, Jesus, Master, have mercy on us. And when he saw them, he said unto them, Go shew yourselves unto the priests. And it came to pass, that, as they went, they were cleansed. And one of them, **when he saw that he was healed, turned back, and with a loud voice***

97

glorified God, and fell down on his face at his feet, giving **him thanks: and he was a Samaritan.** *And Jesus answering said, Were there not ten cleansed? but where are the nine? There are not found that returned to give glory to God, save this stranger. And he said unto him, Arise, go thy way: thy faith hath made thee whole. (Luke 17:13-19)*

The leper that returned to give thanks performed six (6) acts that are note worthy:

1. He recognized that his healing was apparent
2. He reacted immediately – he turned back
3. He made it known to all with a loud voice that he was healed. This sounds like ***GETTO*** worship to me.
4. He fell at Jesus' feet. That looks like someone who just lost his inhibition and his posturing demonstrated that he recognized the lordship of Jesus Christ.
5. A spirit of thankfulness took a hold of him. I believe this is probably how Mary Magdalene felt when she realized she was no longer bound by seven demons.
6. Lastly, he said, I am a ***Samaritan***. People, the man was not legally obliged to be healed, much less entitled to see the priest for cleansing. Just like the woman at the well, Jesus went beyond legalistic barriers to minister to these ten lepers. Hence, their gratitude should have been extraordinary, yet only one returned to give thanks.

Let us pray. Father, we humbly ask that you please open our hearts and minds to what is considered true worship, and more importantly, grant us the will to perform it. These mercies we ask in Jesus' name. Amen!

Insights and Prayer Points for
Praying with praise and worship in your heart.

1. Your *faith* MUST supersede your *flesh* *when doing anything for the Lord.* You live by faith and not by sight. I might add even if you have the wherewithal to supply a need, make it a practice to consult with the Lord first in all your dealings. You will make better decisions, you will derive greater testimonies, and your praise to the Lord will increase. Abraham, Isaac and Jacob were very wealthy, but they understood where their power came from to give them wealth. Adopt the same principle and you too will be successful in giving glory to God.
2. Practice to be thankful!
3. Reject selfishness and embrace altruism.
4. Be a *"get-to"* worshiper, and you will see how your life will shew forth His praises.

Conclusion

As stated in my introduction, I wanted to share what the Lord placed in my heart during my personal prayer about the five principles of POWERful prayers, which are

- *P*ray with passion
- *O*penly confess your convictions
- *W*ork the WORD
- *E*xpect the unexpected
- *R*emember, God Gets the Glory!

My intention was to add another rung to the prayer ladder that leads to the throne of God. I hope something was written that resonated in your heart and mind. I ask if this book did not meet your needs at this time, please don't discard it but rather donate it to a public library or even leave in a thrift shop so someone who might need an easy read can at least reach for my book on prayer. If, however, the words from the pages spoke to your heart even in the smallest way, I ask that you share it with someone else and help to share my passion for praying powerful prayers. And above all, please continue to pray for me that the Lord will make me into a true "*getto*" worshipper. ***Psssss (If you are simply reading the back of my book to see what this is all about and think negatively of my choice of words to describe worshipper, then you MUST read the book. Sorry cannot tell you, my lips are sealed, but this book is opened in your hand, read it, you might be surprised!)*** Let us pray…

Dear Lord, I pray for your people today who might be going through situations that do not seem to have an end.

Please let them know that you would never lead them where you cannot feed them, because you are the Good Shepherd, and a good shepherd will do whatever it takes to find pasture for his sheep. Lord, remember those who feel discouraged, distressed, depressed, disgusted, and are in despair. I send Your ministering Spirit to speak peace and comfort to their hurting hearts. Heal the broken hearted, set the captive free, and wipe away the tears. Be their Strong Refuge and let your undergirding Arms be felt as you carry them. Peace Speaker, please speak comfort to their troubled hearts right now in Jesus' name. Amen!

Let us worship Him for hearing our prayers right now in Jesus' name! Amen and Amen!

God bless you!

About the Author - Margaret R. Banks

The highest call in ministry is the call to pray. Margaret believes that there are no limits, peaks or caps upon God's ability regardless of your challenges. Prayer is man's umbilical cord to God, if severed man is doomed for destruction.

Margaret is the Prayer Coordinator for New York Metro District of the United Pentecostal Church International. She has been in Christian service for some 30 years, and is extensively involved in all areas of ministry. She has a strong desire to be mightily used of God and has positioned herself to leave an indelible mark upon this generation. She is a sought after speaker, and travels nationally and internationally ministering to the body of Christ. She is an integral member of the Oneness Rehoboth Apostolic Church in Mt. Vernon, NY under the able leadership of Bishop Arthur Thomas, where she directs the Prayer Ministry, and heads the Evangelism Ministries.

Margaret is an Adjunct Professor at two colleges in New York City. Professor Banks holds a Master of Science in Organizational Leadership with Distinction, a Bachelor of Science in Business Administration, Cum Laude, and is a member of the Delta Mu Delta Society, an International Honor Society in Business Administration for high scholastic attainment, and has been elected a member of Beta Upsilon Chapter – Mercy College.

Let us remain faithful to our Lord Jesus Christ, because at the end of all things we want to hear, *"Well done thou good and faithful servant, enter thou into the joy of the Lord."*
That's my prayer!

References

A Bottle of Spikenard, very costly -
www.agsconsulting.com/htdbv5/r2447.htm

Baker Books, The Complete Works of E.M>Bounds on Prayer, pg.13.
Prince Press, June 2002

Concordance with Hebrew and Greek Lexicon.

Holy Bible—all scriptures taken from King James ·Version unless
otherwise noted.

http://www.eliyah.com/lexicon.html

Spikenard, *http://healinghandsapothecary.com/Spikenard.html*

Spurgeon. Charles. "Confession of the Mouth" July 19, 1863
http://www.scribd.com/doc/23470834/Confession-With-the-Mouth-Charles-H-Spurgeon

Webster's New World Dictionary, 2nd College Edition, 1979, published
by Simon & Schuster, New York, NY

Wurmbrand, Richard. "Tortured For Christ" 1965, 1967 Published by
Diane Books, USA

www.Wikipedia.com

Order Request

To place an order or to leave a comment, please go to my
website

http://www.margaretbanks.tk

If you have any questions, feel free to call me at
(914) 582-5277

Shalom!